WINE ROAD
NORTHERN SONOMA COUNTY

tasting along the wine road

cookbook

foreword by Luis Rodriguez

tasting along
the wine road

cookbook

a collection of recipes from
"A Wine & Food Affair"

cookbook **volume 12**

Recipes from the Wineries and Lodgings of the
Alexander, Dry Creek and Russian River Valleys.

WINE ROAD
NORTHERN SONOMA COUNTY

A custom cookbook published by

Wine Road Northern Sonoma County

P.O. Box 46, Healdsburg, CA 95448

www.wineroad.com

Content © Wine Road Northern Sonoma County

Design © Pembroke Studios, www.pembrokestudios.com

Editor Linda Murphy, linda@lindamurphywine.com

Bottle shot photography © Kelly McManus, www.kellymcmanusphotography.com

Lodging photography © Lenny Siegel, www.siegelphotographic.com

Cover photography © Dustin Costa

ISBN 978-1-4507-1862-2

Printed in China

table of contents

table of contents

table of contents

foreword

executive chef Luis Rodriguez

Equus Restaurant, Santa Rosa, CA

My love for food started at a young age, when I would sit beside my mother and help her make pastry. She had a passion for cooking and I knew that I would follow in her footsteps. Through her encouragement, I would experiment in the kitchen, creating meals for our family from the freshest ingredients I could find.

After 20 years of working in corporate kitchens throughout the United States, I stumbled upon a hidden gem in Northern California … Sonoma County.

After my first stroll through a local farmer's market, I was hooked! Fresh tomatoes, beans, artisan cheeses, honey and meat – it was all here. I knew then that this would be my home and the place where I would continue cooking. That was more than 10 years ago, and not a day goes by where I don't think about how lucky I am to be a chef in this little slice of heaven.

At Equus Restaurant, our seasonal menu reflects the bounty of Sonoma County. Our fish is delivered fresh daily from Bodega Bay. Tomatoes arrive from a farm in Alexander Valley. Herbs are cultivated in a small, sunny patch on our property. Fresh food simply tastes better, especially when it is paired with Sonoma County wines. Our menu changes every three months and reflects what is fresh and in season in our region – the way it should be.

I know my fellow Sonoma County chefs feel as fortunate as I do to be living and cooking in such a culinary mecca. I hope that visitors have the opportunity to visit our award-winning wineries, taste some delicious food, and enjoy all that Sonoma County has to offer.

recipes
from the wineries & lodgings

brunch

Camellia Inn

211 north street
healdsburg, ca 95448
707-433-8182

www.camelliainn.com

At the Camellia Inn, we love chocolate, so
every Wednesday we cover our guests,
inside and out, with chocolate soap,
chocolate treats, chocolate body paint, and
for breakfast, a chocolate dish. This is a
favorite on the following morning, as part
of our "Chocolate Covered Wednesdays."
We describe it as a "baked crepe" to
our guests. The recipe is adapted from
"Morning Food" by Margaret S. Fox.

Serves 4

chocolate covered wednesdays'

chocolate-cherry clafouti

chef Lucy Lewand

ingredients

¾ cup mini chocolate chips
2 cups pitted cherries
3 eggs
1 cup plus 2 tablespoons sugar
½ cup plus 1 tablespoon flour
1 cup plus 2 tablespoons heavy cream
1 stick butter
pinch of salt
powdered sugar, for sprinkling

directions preheat oven to 400°

Grease 2 10-inch quiche pans and arrange the chocolate chips and cherries evenly in the bottom of the pans.

Combine the eggs, sugar, flour, cream and salt in a food processor and blend until smooth. Pour ¼ of the mixture into each of the 2 quiche pans, reserving the remaining half. Bake for 15 minutes and remove from the oven.

In a small saucepan, melt the stick of butter, let it cool slightly, then add it to the food processor with the remaining batter. Blend until mixed. Pour the buttery batter on top of the partially baked mixture in the quiche pans, and bake for another 15 minutes. Cool 10 minutes, sprinkle with powdered sugar and serve.

Note: Although cherries and chocolate are a fabulous combination, you can substitute another fruit, and even skip the chocolate chips.

pair with korbel moscato frizzante

Case Ranch Inn

7446 poplar drive
forestville, ca 95436
707-887-8711

www.caseranchinn.com

This frittata consistently receives rave reviews from our guests, especially when we use the fresh zucchini and basil from our organic summer vegetable garden. It can be made year-round, with fresh produce from your local market. Accompany this frittata with roasted potatoes and you have a hearty breakfast.

Serves 8-10

zucchini basil frittata

chef Diana Van Ry

ingredients

2 teaspoons olive oil
2 cups zucchini squash, diced
½ cup all-purpose flour
1 teaspoon baking powder
10 eggs, lightly beaten
1 tablespoon vegetable oil
2 cups small-curd non-fat cottage cheese
½ cup fresh basil, chopped (or 2 tablespoons dried)
½ pound Monterey Jack cheese, grated

directions preheat oven to 350°

Butter or lightly oil a 9-inch by 13-inch shallow baking dish. In a large skillet over medium heat, heat the olive oil. Add the zucchini and sauté for several minutes, stirring so the zucchini does not brown. Turn off the heat and allow the squash to cool.

In a large bowl, mix the flour and baking powder. Add the eggs and vegetable oil, blending well. Blend in the remaining ingredients, gradually adding and incorporating the warm zucchini in the bowl.

Put the mixture into the prepared baking dish and bake for 35-45 minutes, or until set. The frittata is done when a knife or toothpick inserted into the center comes out dry. Let stand for about 5 minutes, then cut into squares and serve hot.

George Alexander House

423 matheson street
healdsburg, ca 95448
707-433-1358

www.georgealexanderhouse.com

This is a recipe that can be used for a spread on homemade buttermilk biscuits or as a dessert in phyllo cups with fresh berries. It is easy to make and so much better than store bought. The curd can be prepared 2 days ahead.

Makes 2 cups

lemon curd

chef Holly Schatz

vegi

ingredients

1 cup sugar
3 large eggs
1 egg yolk
1 cup unsalted butter, cut into pieces
6 tablespoons fresh lemon juice
2 tablespoons lemon zest

directions

In a heavy saucepan over low heat, whisk in all the ingredients until the butter melts. Cook until the mixture thickens to the consistency of lightly whipped cream, whisking constantly for about 10 minutes.

Cover and refrigerate until cold (about 4 hours).

Hope-Merrill House & Hope-Bosworth House

21253 geyserville avenue
geyserville, ca 95441
707-857-3356

www.hope-inns.com

At our two inns, one dish stands out with our guests: Lemon Soufflé Pancakes. We like to jazz them up, depending on our whim, with various add-ons to the batter, including chopped bananas, chopped papayas, grated apples and fresh berries.
Be creative with your own additions.

Serves 4-6

lemon
soufflé pancakes

chef **Cosette Trautman-Scheiber**

ingredients

6 eggs, separated
2 cups small-curd cottage cheese
¼ cup vegetable oil
2 tablespoons maple syrup or granulated sugar
½ teaspoon salt
4 teaspoons freshly squeezed lemon juice
4 teaspoons baking powder
1 cup unbleached all-purpose flour

directions preheat a griddle or large heavy skillet

In a bowl, beat the egg whites until they're stiff but not dry. Set aside.

In a food processor or blender, add the cottage cheese, egg yolks, oil, maple syrup/sugar, salt, lemon juice, baking powder and flour, and blend until smooth. Fold in the egg whites.

Lightly oil the griddle/skillet, and spoon on the batter, about 3 tablespoons for each pancake, and bake until the tops are bubbly. Turn the pancakes and cook them until their bottoms are done. Serve hot with your favorite toppings.

Inn at Occidental

3657 church street
occidental, ca 95465
707-874-1047

www.innatoccidental.com

Tina had been seeking an exciting
breakfast dish that incorporates the prior
day's croissants, which at times go to waste.
She came up with this pudding, and we're
often asked for the recipe by our guests. We
use fresh apples – after all, this area is still
known for its apples, and our neighboring
community of Sebastopol celebrates the
Apple Blossom Festival every year.

Serves 8

fresh apple
croissant pudding

chef Tina Wolsborn

ingredients

½ tablespoon unsalted butter
1 large Granny Smith apple, peeled & diced
1 cinnamon stick
2 tablespoons light brown sugar, packed
½ cup apple juice
5 cups croissants, cut into ½-inch cubes (about 3-4 croissants)
1 cup heavy cream
2 large eggs
¼ cup plus 1 tablespoon granulated sugar

directions preheat oven to 375°; position rack in middle of oven

Melt the butter in a 10-inch heavy skillet over moderate heat. Add the apples and cinnamon, and sauté until the apples are pale golden, about 3 minutes. Add the brown sugar and cook, stirring, until the sugar melts and the apples are slightly caramelized. Add the apple juice and cook over moderate heat, until the apples are tender and the juice has evaporated, about 3 to 4 minutes. Discard the cinnamon.

Spread the apples in the bottom of a 9-inch pie pan. Spread the croissant cubes evenly over the apples.

Whisk together the cream, eggs and ¼ cup of the granulated sugar. Pour the mixture evenly over the croissant cubes, pressing them down slightly to moisten. Sprinkle the top with the remaining granulated sugar and bake, uncovered, until the pudding is set and the top lightly browned, approximately 25 to 30 minutes.

Cool on a rack for 10 minutes and serve warm.

Raford Inn
of Healdsburg

10630 wohler road
healdsburg, ca 95448
707-887-9573

www.rafordinn.com

Guests tell us this is the best quiche
they've ever had. We use the freshest local
vegetables we can find, and sometimes
substitute Fontina, Gouda, Swiss or Gruyere
for the Asiago cheese. Feel free to blend
various cheeses, to your taste.

Serves 6

garden
vegetable quiche
chef Rita Wells

ingredients

1 tablespoon olive oil
1 medium onion, chopped
½ bell pepper (any color), chopped
1 small zucchini, sliced
1 small yellow or crookneck squash, sliced
3 large fresh Swiss chard leaves, chopped
5 large fresh basil leaves, chopped
6 eggs
1 cup skim milk
½ cup Asiago cheese, grated
1 teaspoon garlic salt
¼ teaspoon pepper
1 medium tomato, thinly wedged
¼ cup parmesan cheese, grated
1 9-inch uncooked pie shell

directions preheat oven to 375°

In a large skillet, heat the olive oil and sauté the onion, bell pepper, zucchini and yellow squash until the vegetables are tender (do not brown). Add the chard and basil, cover the skillet, and steam the ingredients until the leaves and stems of the chard are tender (about 5 minutes).

While the vegetables cook, in a medium bowl, mix the eggs, milk, Asiago, garlic salt and pepper. When the vegetables are done, pour the egg mixture into the pie crust and add the steamed veggies. Top with the tomato wedges and sprinkle with parmesan cheese.

Bake for 30 to 35 minutes, until a knife inserted in the center of the quiche comes out clean. Let stand 5 minutes before serving.

Santa Nella House B & B

12130 highway 116
guerneville, ca 95446
707-869-9488

www.santanellahouse.com

The original recipe for this dish did not
use blackberries, but with the abundance
of this fruit in our area, we pick them fresh
off the bushes in our yard. Our guests
love to help in the harvest, knowing that
the next morning they will taste
the fruits of their labor.

Serves 4

blackberry kuchen

chef Bob Reeves

ingredients

Topping
¼ cup brown sugar, packed
¼ cup sugar
¼ cup flour
¼ cup graham cracker crumbs
3 tablespoons cold butter, cut into chunks

Kuchen
1 egg, beaten well
½ cup sugar
½ cup milk
2 tablespoons vegetable oil
1 cup flour
2 teaspoons baking soda
1 cup blackberries, fresh or frozen
1 teaspoon cinnamon

directions preheat oven to 375°

To prepare the topping, combine the first 4 ingredients in a bowl. Cut in the butter until you have coarse crumbs. Place the mixture in the refrigerator until ready for use.

To prepare the kuchen, in a bowl, combine the egg, sugar, milk and oil, and mix well. In a separate bowl, sift together the flour and baking powder. Add this to the egg mixture and blend well.

Grease an 8-inch-square pan, and add the mixture. In a small bowl, blend the blackberries and cinnamon. Sprinkle the berry blend over the batter, and scatter the topping over the blackberries. Bake for 25 to 30 minutes, until a knife inserted into the center of the cake is clean. Serve warm.

Sonoma Orchid Inn

12850 river road
guerneville, ca 95446
707-887-1033

www.sonomaorchidinn.com

These cakes are delicious as is, but because we also eat with our eyes, I've added an optional step to enhance the presentation. As an extra, blend 2-½ ounces of blackberries (12 to 15) with 1 tablespoon of lemon juice and 3 tablespoons of sugar in a food processor until smooth. Pass the mixture through a fine sieve into a small bowl, discard the solids, and set the liquid aside. Then continue with the recipe.

Serves 6

lemon-blackberry
pudding cakes
chef Dana Murphy

vegi

ingredients

butter for greasing ramekins
4 large eggs, separated
1 cup sugar
6 tablespoons cake flour
1 cup milk
1 pint blackberries
½ cup fresh lemon juice
¼ teaspoon salt
3 tablespoons unsalted butter, melted
1 teaspoon lemon zest (optional)
boiling water for pan
4 ounces crème fraiche (optional)

directions preheat oven to 350°.

Butter 6 10-ounce ramekins and set them aside. In a medium bowl, whisk together the egg yolks and ¾ cup of the sugar. Whisk in the flour and milk in two batches each, beginning with the flour. Whisk in the ½ cup lemon juice, salt, melted butter and lemon zest, if using. Set aside.

Whip the egg whites until they're frothy, and add the remaining ¼ cup sugar slowly, until the egg whites hold stiff but don't form dry peaks. Whisk half the whites into the lemon mixture until combined. Gently fold in the other half.

Place the ramekins in a high-sided roasting pan or baking dish. Put some blackberries in the bottom of the ramekins. Divide the batter among the ramekins, filling each almost to the top. If using the berry sauce explained in the introduction, spoon a few teaspoons of it onto each cake, and use a toothpick to swirl the sauce into a pretty pattern in the batter. Transfer the pan containing the ramekins to the oven, and pour boiling water into the pan until the level reaches halfway up the sides of the ramekins.

Bake the cakes until they are set and their tops are just turning golden brown, 35 to 40 minutes. With tongs, transfer the ramekins from the pan to a wire rack and let them cool for 15 minutes.

If using, beat the crème fraiche in a bowl until it forms soft peaks. Serve the cakes with a dollop of crème fraiche and any remaining blackberries.

appetizers

C. Donatiello Winery

4035 westside road
healdsburg, ca 95448
707-431-4442

www.cdonatiello.com

Tinga is a traditional dish from Mexico and Latin America, comprised of shredded meat or chicken. Deep flavors of smoky chiles, tomatoes and long-simmered spices give tinga its authentic and addictive profile. In this version, Liberty Duck legs and Quetzal Farms chiles marry with shiitake mushrooms and wild arugula to create a truly local take on a classic.

Makes 4 tostadas

duck & shiitake
tinga tostadas
with wild arugula salad & queso fresco

chef Christopher Greenwald, Bay Laurel Culinary

ingredients

2 Liberty Duck legs, roasted, fat and shredded
meat reserved, skin and bones discarded
1 white onion, julienned
¼ pound shiitake mushrooms, stems discarded
and caps sliced
1 clove garlic, minced
1 cup water
2-3 dried red chiles
1 teaspoon tomato paste

¼ cup Pinot Noir
1 teaspoon fresh thyme, minced
1 cup fresh wild arugula, washed and dried
½ teaspoon balsamic vinegar
1 tablespoon extra virgin olive oil
salt to taste
4 corn tostada shells
¼ cup queso fresco, crumbled

directions

Heat the duck fat in a medium saucepan and add the onion. Sauté the onions until they're just tender, add the mushrooms, and sauté until both are cooked down and begin to take on color (no liquid should be in the pan).

In a food processor, add the water and dried red chiles, and purée.

Add to the mushroom mixture the garlic and sauté until just fragrant. Add the tomato paste and chile purée. Cook 5 minutes, stirring, then add the wine. Cook until reduced by half, then add the shredded duck meat. Cook together for a few minutes, then remove from the heat and stir in the thyme. Check for seasoning.

In a medium bowl, toss the arugula with the vinegar, olive oil and salt. To assemble, top each tostada shell with the warm tinga mixture, then arugula salad, then crumbled cheese.

pair with c. donatiello russian river valley pinot noir

Dutcher Crossing Winery

8533 dry creek road
healdsburg, ca 95448
707-431-2711

www.dutchercrossingwinery.com

This simple, rustic and oh-so-satisfying dish always has our wine club members scrambling for seconds during our barrel tastings. Serve it as part of a cozy evening at home, paired with any of our spicy-smooth Zinfandels.

Serves 8

zesty
Fennel & sausage ragu
over risotto with roasted cherry tomatoes

chef Amber Balshaw

ingredients

Risotto
4 tablespoons butter
1 small onion, diced
1 teaspoon dried thyme
4 cloves garlic, crushed
1 cup Arborio rice
1 cup white wine
4 cups chicken or vegetable broth
1 cup grated parmesan cheese

Ragu
1 pound sweet Italian sausage
1 tablespoon fennel seed
1 small onion, diced
4 cloves garlic, crushed
1 tablespoon dry Italian seasoning
¼ cup olive oil
1 15-ounce can crushed tomatoes

Roasted Cherry Tomatoes
1 2-inch rosemary stem
1 basket grape cherry tomatoes
1 tablespoon olive oil
salt and pepper, to taste

directions

To prepare the risotto, add the butter to a large pan and sauté the onions, thyme and garlic over medium-high heat, until they're tender. Add the rice and sauté until well coated, about 1 to 2 minutes. Add the wine, reduce to medium heat, and stir till combined. Add the broth 1 cup at a time, allowing it to be absorbed between batches. This will take 15 to 20 minutes. Season with salt and pepper.

To prepare the ragu, place the first 6 ingredients in a heavy-bottomed sauté pan over medium heat. Cook until the sausage is nicely brown; you can choose the texture of the ragu by how much you macerate the meat. Add the tomatoes and simmer for 15 to 20 minutes, until the liquid evaporates.

To prepare the tomatoes, preheat the oven to 300°. Strip the rosemary from its stem. Place all the ingredients on a baking sheet and mix to coat. Bake for 10 to 12 minutes, until the tomatoes burst.

To serve, place 1 cup of risotto on a plate or bowl, top with ½ cup of the ragu, and finish with cherry tomatoes and freshly grated parmesan.

pair with dutcher crossing zinfandel

Dutton-Goldfield Winery

3100 gravenstein highway north
sebastopol, ca 95472
707-823-3887

www.duttongoldfield.com

I was visiting Rick at Bruno's one evening and happened to open a bottle of the Dutton-Goldfield Freestone Pinot Noir. I had Rick taste it and he remarked how the rich earthiness and lingering spicy notes would beautifully complement the crostini he was serving that night. A few tweaks to the recipe, and a marriage was arranged!

Serves 6

wild mushroom & brie
crostini

chef Rick Bruno, Bruno's On Fourth

vegi

ingredients

1 loaf ciabatta bread
2 tablespoons olive oil plus more for brushing crostini
salt and pepper, to taste
3 ounces portabella mushrooms, sliced
3 ounces chanterelle mushrooms, sliced
3 ounces bolete or other field mushrooms, sliced
½ tablespoon garlic, chopped
½ tablespoon shallots, chopped
½ tablespoon parsley, chopped
½ tablespoon thyme, minced
6 ounces Brie, sliced

directions preheat a grill

Slice the ciabatta into 6 ¼-inch-thick slices and brush both sides with olive oil. Lightly season with salt and pepper and grill the bread until it's golden brown. Set aside.

Preheat a large sauté pan and add the 2 tablespoons of oil. Stir in all the mushrooms and sauté until golden brown. Add the garlic, shallots, parsley and thyme to the pan and continue to sauté until the shallots are soft.

To assemble the crostini, place a slice of Brie on top of a slice of grilled bread, add a dollop of the mushroom mixture, and enjoy.

pair with dutton-goldfield freestone hill pinot noir

Holdredge Winery

51 front street
healdsburg, ca 95448
707-431-1424

www.holdredgewine.com

These delicious little hors d'oeuvres are quick, easy to make and very popular. Be sure you prepare lots of them! The combination of sweet, spicy, salty and smoky makes them a great match for Holdredge Pinot Noir. The optional Pinot Noir balsamic glaze recipe makes 2 cups and can be used with many other dishes.

Makes 36 pieces

bacon-wrapped dates

with chorizo & balsamic glaze

chef Bruce Riezenman, Park Avenue Catering

ingredients

Dates

12 slices best quality bacon you can find
3 links chorizo sausage (moderately spicy)
36 Medjool dates, pits removed
36 fancy bamboo toothpicks
2 tablespoons Pinot Noir-balsamic glaze (optional)

Pinot Noir Balsamic Glaze

1 tablespoon butter
1/4 cup shallots, finely diced
1 tablespoon golden brown sugar
1/2 cup Pinot Noir
2 quarts balsamic vinegar

directions preheat oven to 350°

To prepare the dates, place a medium-sized sauce pot over high heat with 1-½ quarts of water. When the water boils, lower to a simmer and add the bacon slices, 1 at a time, so that they don't stick together. Simmer for 3 to 5 minutes, remove the bacon, and lay the slices out on a paper towel.

Roast the chorizo in the oven for 10 to 15 minutes. This renders some of the fat. Remove the links and let them cool. Remove the skins and cut the chorizo into rectangles just large enough to tightly replace the pit in the dates.

Insert the chorizo strips into each date. Lay out the bacon slices side by side on a cutting board. Roll a bacon slice tightly around the first date so that it is 2 layers thick. This should use 1/3 to 1/2 of the slice. Cut the bacon at that point and place a toothpick through the bacon and date to hold it together. Using this technique, you should be able to roll 2 or 3 dates from each slice of bacon. Continue until all the dates are rolled. You can do this the day before.

To serve, place the bacon-rolled dates on a baking sheet and roast for approximately 15 minutes, until the bacon is crisp on the outside. Drizzle very lightly with balsamic glaze and watch them disappear.

To prepare the glaze, sauté the shallots in butter in a saucepan. Add the brown sugar and wine and cook, reducing the mixture by half. Strain the sauce to remove the shallots.

Add the balsamic vinegar, bring the sauce to a boil, and turn on the exhaust fan. As the sauce starts to thicken, lower the heat and slowly reduce it to 1 cup. The resulting liquid will be thick, shiny and smooth. Use chilled or at room temperature; this sauce will last for weeks.

pair with holdredge russian river valley pinot noir

J. Keverson Winery

53 front street
healdsburg, ca 95448
707-433-3097

www.jkeverson.com

I'm always looking for ways to serve familiar foods in small bites. This take on a steak sandwich comes in handy when you prepare all the components ahead of time. Then it's all ready to assemble for easy appetizers on the bocce court or enjoying on a beautiful fall evening on the patio.

Makes 25 pieces

zinfandel-marinated
tri-tip on bruschetta
with caramelized onions & roasted garlic dressing

chef Diane Bard

ingredients

Tri-Tip
2-½ pounds beef tri-tip
2 cups J. Keverson Buck Hill Zinfandel
½ cup Worcestershire sauce
4 tablespoons balsamic vinegar
4 tablespoons extra virgin olive oil
(we like Terra Bella Vista)
4 tablespoons fresh rosemary, chopped
4 cloves garlic, minced
sea salt and pepper, to taste

Caramelized Onions
3 tablespoons extra virgin olive oil
2 large yellow sweet onions, thinly sliced
2 tablespoons red wine vinegar
sea salt
½ teaspoon freshly ground black pepper
1 tablespoon fresh thyme, chopped

Dressing
1 cup good-quality mayonnaise
¼ cup sour cream
2 teaspoons Dijon mustard
2 teaspoons white balsamic vinegar
1 head roasted garlic
½ teaspoon freshly ground black pepper
salt, to taste
1/2 tablespoon fresh thyme, minced

Assembly
1 French bread baguette
extra virgin olive oil
sea salt and ground black pepper, to taste
2 cups arugula, julienned

directions marinate the meat 1 day ahead

To prepare the tri-tip, place it in a large zip-lock bag, add the remaining ingredients, squish the bag to mix the contents, and refrigerate overnight.

To prepare the dressing, in a medium bowl, whisk the mayonnaise, sour cream, mustard and vinegar until well incorporated. Squeeze the roasted garlic from the head and smash with the side of a knife blade. Stir in the garlic, pepper, salt and thyme, and refrigerate until ready to use.

To prepare the onions, in a large skillet, heat the olive oil over medium-high heat. Add the onions and cook, stirring often, for 3 minutes. Turn down the heat to low and continue to cook for about 20 minutes, until the onions are soft and light golden. Allow to cool (can be made 1 day ahead).

Preheat the oven to 350°. Place the beef and marinade in a baking dish and roast in the oven until done (120° for medium-rare). Remove the dish from the oven, cover with foil, and let the tri-tip rest for 15 minutes. Cut into ¼-inch slices. Set the oven to broil.

Slice the bread on the diagonal into ¼-inch thick slices. Brush olive oil on each slice and sprinkle with salt and pepper. Place the slices on a baking sheet and broil until they're slightly golden, 1 to 2 minutes.

To assemble, top each slice of baguette with dressing, a slice of beef, a sprinkling of arugula, and some of the caramelized onion. Serve right away.

pair with j. keverson buck hill zinfandel

Kendall-Jackson, Healdsburg

337 healdsburg avenue
healdsburg, ca 95448
707-433-7102

www.kj.com

Is there any other ingredient that shouts "fall" and "holidays" louder than pumpkin? It can be used in so many ways, both savory and sweet, and we love pumpkin as a filling for quesadillas. This recipe uses ham hock and Carmody cow's milk cheese from Sonoma County's Bellwether Farms. Carmody melts beautifully and has a buttery flavor and texture – perfect for Chardonnay.

Serves 8

ham hock & carmody
quesadilla
with roasted pumpkin

ingredients

2 tablespoons butter
1 tablespoon fresh thyme, minced
2 cups pumpkin, cut into ¼-inch dice
1 tablespoon kosher salt
1 ham hock
8 flour tortillas
16 ounces Carmody cheese, grated

directions preheat oven to 350°

To prepare the pumpkin, place an oven-proof pan in the preheated oven for 10 minutes. Add the butter, thyme and pumpkin, and season with salt. Roast the pumpkin until it's golden brown and tender, about 15 minutes. Remove the pumpkin from the oven and let cool. Add salt, to taste.

To prepare the ham hock, in a 2-quart saucepan, add 1 quart of cold water and the hock, and place the pan over high heat. When the water boils, reduce the heat to low, cover and simmer until the meat is tender, about 3 hours. When the meat is done, remove and reserve the ham hock at room temperature and strain the broth into a container. Chill the broth overnight and reserve for another use.

Once the ham hock is cool enough to handle, pick and save all the meat, discarding all bone, skin and cartilage, then refrigerate.

When you're ready to serve the quesadillas, cover half of each tortilla with 2 ounces of the grated cheese, 1 ounce of ham hock meat and 3 tablespoons of roasted pumpkin. Fold each tortilla in half and press firmly. Toast both sides of the quesadilla in a hot nonstick pan until the tortillas turn golden brown. Serve hot.

pair with kendall-jackson jackson hills chardonnay

Kendall-Jackson Wine Center

5007 fulton road
fulton, ca 95439
707-571-8100

www.kj.com

For these flatbreads, we grill radicchio and combine it with Medjool dates to offset the slight bitterness of the radicchio; smoked mozzarella and fresh rosemary make each bite and sip of wine more exciting than the last.

Makes 6 pieces

radicchio & medjool

pizzetta

with smoked mozzarella

chef Taki Laliotitis

ingredients

Dough
1-½ cups warm water
2 teaspoons dried yeast
4 cups high-gluten flour plus ¼ cup for flouring
2 tablespoons kosher salt

Pizzetta
¼ cup extra virgin olive oil
1-½ cups scamorza (smoked mozzarella), grated

Radicchio & Medjool Mix
2 garlic cloves, minced
¼ teaspoon rosemary, minced
¼ teaspoon thyme, minced
2 tablespoons balsamic vinegar
2 tablespoons vegetable oil
2 heads radicchio, each quartered
1 cup Medjool dates, pitted
¼ cup balsamic vinegar
salt and pepper, to taste

directions preheat grill to 500°; preheat oven to 475°

To prepare the dough, mix the water and yeast in a mixing bowl. Add the flour, then the salt, keeping the ingredients separate. Do not mix. Allow the yeast to activate and create bubbles.

When you see this, mix the dough in an electric mixer, using a dough hook attachment. Mix until well incorporated, about 5 to 8 minutes. If the dough is wet, add flour until the dough pulls away from the side of the bowl. Cover the bowl with plastic wrap and allow it to rise until it doubles in size. Punch down the dough and divide it into 4 equal balls. Cover the dough and allow it to rise for another 20 to 30 minutes.

To prepare the radicchio, heat a grill to medium-high. Place the garlic, rosemary, thyme, 2 tablespoons of balsamic vinegar, oil and quartered radicchio in a large bowl. Season with salt and pepper, and toss together. Let rest for 5 minutes.

Grill the radicchio pieces well on all sides, then place them on a cutting board. Remove the core of the radicchio so that the leaves fall apart. Rough-chop the leaves and place them into a bowl.

Quarter the dates and mix with the second portion of vinegar to prevent the dates from sticking. Pour the mixture into a 12-inch sauté pan. Bring the mixture to a simmer, and add the radicchio. Cook until the vinegar has almost gone dry, remove the pan from the heat, and chill the mixture immediately. Season with salt and pepper.

When the dough has rested, flour a work surface and roll out a ball of dough to 12 to 14 inches in diameter. Shake off the excess flour and place the dough in a baking pan. Brush the dough with extra virgin olive oil. Spread the radicchio/date mixture over the dough. Lightly cover with the smoked mozzarella and bake the pizzetta in the oven for 6 to 8 minutes. Remove the pan from the oven and cut the pizzetta into 6 pieces.

pair with seco highlands pinot noir

La Crema
Tasting Room

235 healdsburg avenue
healdsburg, ca 95448
707-431-9400

www.lacrema.com

We're fortunate to have one of the best poultry purveyors in the country in our area, Sonoma County Poultry. Whenever we prepare duck dishes, the company's Liberty brand is our choice. Saba – reduced grape juice – is available at most gourmet grocery stores; if you can't find it, substitute with honey or molasses.

Serves 8

liberty duck confit

bruschetta

with swiss chard, shallots & pine nuts

ingredients

Duck Confit

6 Liberty Duck legs, thighs attached
½ pound kosher salt
5 sprigs thyme
1 tablespoon black peppercorns, whole
1 tablespoon fennel seed
1 bay leaf
1 tablespoon juniper berries
1 quart duck fat

Swiss Chard Bruschetta

9 ounces Swiss chard
3 ounces shallots, sliced into ½-inch rings
1 large garlic clove, crushed and chopped
½ teaspoon fresh thyme, chopped
1 tablespoon olive oil
kosher salt and black pepper, to taste
8 slices crusty ciabatta bread
½ tablespoon balsamic vinegar
½ teaspoon saba
1 tablespoon pine nuts, toasted

directions start the confit 1 day ahead

Place the duck legs in a pan. Coat the legs with salt and all the other ingredients, except for the duck fat. Place the pan in the refrigerator overnight.

The next day, preheat the oven to 275°. Rinse the duck with running water and pat the legs dry with paper towels. Place the duck in an oven-proof pan and cover with the duck fat. Cover the pan with foil and place it in the oven. Cook until the duck is tender and falling off of the bone.

Remove the pan from the oven, let the meat cool, pick it off the bones and shred it with your fingers or 2 forks.

To prepare the bruschetta, preheat a grill to high. Separate the stems and leaves of the Swiss chard. In a bowl, mix the chard stems, leaves, shallots, garlic, thyme and olive oil. Season with salt and pepper.

Starting with the chard stems and shallots, grill them until they're soft and lightly caramelized, 1 to 1½ minutes, and transfer to a large plate. Grill the chard leaves for approximately 45 seconds, until they're wilted and slightly charred, and remove them to the plate. Lightly grill the bread, until grill marks appear.

Place the chard stems and leaves on a cutting board and chop them into ½-inch pieces. In a sauté pan, add the chard, balsamic vinegar and saba. Cook briefly over high heat, until the liquid reduces and coats all of the ingredients.

To serve, spoon the mixture onto the grilled bread, sprinkle with pine nuts, and top with the duck.

pair with la crema russian river valley pinot noir

La Crema Winery

3690 laughlin road
windsor, ca 95492
707-571-1504

www.lacrema.com

Pinot Noir is the ideal wine to unlock the flavors in this dish. The dark red fruit and touch of spice in Carneros Pinot Noir draw out the plum profile in the meatballs.

Serves 8-10

lamb meatballs

with prunes

chef Taki Laliotis

ingredients

1 pound ground lamb
¼ teaspoon ground cinnamon
1 teaspoon fresh thyme, finely chopped
2 tablespoons parsley, finely chopped
4 mint leaves, chopped
⅔ cup onion, minced
½ teaspoon garlic, minced
¼ cup prunes, diced
salt and pepper
¼ cup vegetable oil

directions preheat oven to 400°

In a large bowl, place the lamb, cinnamon, thyme, parsley, mint, onion, garlic and prunes and gently mix. Season with salt and pepper. Test the batch for seasoning by pan-frying a small piece of the meat mixture. Adjust the seasoning if necessary. Form the meatballs using a large ice cream scoop, with approximately 3 ounces of meat per scoop.

Place a 10-inch sauté pan over medium heat. Add the vegetable oil, and brown the meatballs on all sides. Place them in a casserole dish, and finish the meatballs in the oven for approximately 8 to 10 minutes, or until they are cooked through. Remove from the oven and allow to cool before serving.

pair with la crema los carneros pinot noir

Lynmar Estate

3909 frei road
sebastopol, ca 95472
707-829-3374

www.lynmarestate.com

The gardeners at Lynmar are committed to promoting endangered heirloom varieties. The leek variety Ester Cook is one of these, and our kitchen gardener, Sara McCamant, grew these leeks just for this event. This recipe also highlights some of the world-class food being produced in our area, including Karen Bianchi-Moreda's Estero Gold from Valley Ford Cheese Company, and Beth Thorp's Nightingale Bakery in Forestville.

Serves 36, as small wedges

ester cook heirloom
leek panini
with estero gold cheese and nightingale bread

chef Sandra Simile

ingredients

4 to 6 large Ester Cook leeks (or similar), roots and dark green tops removed
3 tablespoons butter
⅓ cup Chardonnay
½ cup vegetable stock
½ teaspoon kosher salt
¼ teaspoon black pepper, freshly ground
3 tablespoons lemon thyme, finely chopped
8 ounces Estero Gold cheese, or a medium Gouda or Asiago
12 slices seeded sourdough bread from Nightingale Bakery, or a white artisan loaf
1 to 2 tablespoons olive oil

directions

Cut the leeks in half lengthwise and rinse them to remove any dirt. Slice the leeks thinly; you should have 5 cups.

Sauté the leeks in the butter on very low heat for 20 to 25 minutes, until they're soft. Don't let them brown. When the leeks are soft, add the Chardonnay and cook for 3 minutes. Add the stock and cook 3 minutes more.

Add the salt, pepper and lemon thyme, and cook until all the liquid is gone and the leeks are barely moist. Cool to room temperature.

Preheat a panini grill to high. Assemble the panini by equally distributing the leeks on 6 slices of bread. Top each with 1/6 of the cheese and then a slice of bread. Lightly brush the sandwiches with oil, and grill them until the cheese melts and the bread is lightly toasted. Cool for a minute and cut into 6 wedges as an hors d'oeuvre or in half if serving as a sandwich.

pair with lynmar russian river valley chardonnay

Martin Ray
Winery

2191 laguna road
santa rosa, ca 95401
707-823-2404

www.martinraywinery.com

Sliders of all sorts are very popular these days. Most of the work can be done the day before, so all you have to do when your guests arrive is to serve a basket of small slider buns, a bowl of warmed Cabernet pulled pork, and a bowl of Cabernet onions. The trick is long, slow cooking of the pork. The shoulder has plenty of fat to keep it moist and tender through the cooking process.

Makes 25-30 hors d'oeuvres

pulled pork sliders
with cabernet caramelized onions

chef Bruce Riezenman, Park Avenue Catering

ingredients

Pork
4-to 5-pound pork shoulder, boneless
1 cup Cabernet Sauvignon
5 garlic cloves, peeled and sliced
2 sprigs fresh rosemary
1 ripe Santa Rosa (or other) dark plum,
pit removed and chopped
1 tablespoon whole grain mustard
10 grinds black pepper
¼ cup olive oil
salt, to taste

Caramelized Onions
4 medium red onions, peeled and thinly sliced
2 cups Cabernet Sauvignon
¼ cup sugar
1 bay leaf
pinch salt
8 mint leaves, finely chopped
30 small slider buns (the smallest you can get)

directions marinate the pork overnight

To prepare the pork, purchase a boneless shoulder that is tied up as a roast in a "net."

In a glass baking dish, combine all the ingredients and marinate the pork "open" overnight by removing the net. Turn the meat a few times during the marinating process.

The next day, place the pork back in the net. If you have a rotisserie, skewer the shoulder on the spit and cook it over low heat for 3 to 4 hours, with a pan underneath to catch the drippings, until the meat is tender enough to be easily pulled apart. It should be golden brown and nicely crisp on the outside.

If you have a grill with a cover, start a small fire of coals (or gas fire) on the outer ends of the barbecue and place the meat in the middle, with no flame directly below it, and cook for the same amount of time as above. It should cook at a temperature of around 200-225°.

You can also slow-cook the pork in the oven at the lowest setting (175-250°). Cover the baking dish containing the pork and marinade for the first 2 hours; remove the cover, turn the oven to 275°, and cook until the pork is very tender.

Remove the pork from the heat, allow it to cool, and pull the meat apart. Remove the fat from the drippings pan and place the meat back in the juice that has accumulated. Allow the pork to cool until you can easily touch it. You can chill it and reheat 2 to 3 days later.

To prepare the onions, in a small heavy-bottomed sauce pot, place the onions, wine, sugar and bay leaves. Cover tightly and simmer for 15 minutes on medium-high heat. Uncover the onions and continue cooking for about 45 minutes, stirring occasionally, until most of the liquid has evaporated. When the onions cool, mix in the mint.

To assemble the sliders, add 1 spoonful each of the pork and onions to the bun, and enjoy.

pair with martin ray cabernet sauvignon

Moshin Vineyards

10295 westside road
healdsburg, ca 95448
707-433-5499

www.moshinvineyards.com

If you've been lucky enough to have tasted this salmon at the winery, then you understand why we call it "famous." Smoking the salmon with Pinot Noir–soaked grape or fruitwood chips lends a delicate smokiness to the fish while keeping it moist.

Makes 20 cups

rick's famous
smoked salmon
in phyllo cups

chef Dan Lucia, DL Catering

ingredients

Smoked Salmon
½ cup soy sauce
½ cup water
1 tablespoon garlic salt
1 tablespoon brown sugar
1 tablespoon smoked paprika
1 tablespoon black pepper
1 tablespoon thyme
1 large (3-pound) salmon fillet

Phyllo Cups
3 tablespoons fresh orange juice
2 tablespoons golden balsamic vinegar
2 teaspoons Dijon mustard
2 tablespoons shallots, finely diced
⅓ cup olive oil
1 head romaine lettuce, julienned
salt and pepper, to taste
1 2-ounce jar capers, drained
8 ounces crème fraiche
20 phyllo cups, baked
12 ounces Rick's Famous Smoked Salmon,
crumbled

directions marinate the salmon 1 day ahead

To prepare the smoked salmon, combine the first 7 ingredients in a large zip-lock plastic bag.
Place the salmon fillet in the bag and allow it to marinate in the refrigerator overnight.

Stack charcoal briquettes in a barbecue grill and ignite. Meanwhile, soak 1 pound of fruitwood
chips – or Pinot Noir grapewood chips, if you have them – in 2 to 3 cups of Pinot Noir for 20
minutes. When the charcoal is ready, drop the chips on the glowing coals.

Place the salmon on grill, away from direct heat, and close the grill cover. Cook the salmon until
it's done and the smoke has properly flavored the fish, about 30 minutes to 1 hour.

To prepare the phyllo cups, in a small jar, combine the orange juice, golden balsamic vinegar,
Dijon mustard, shallots and olive oil. Seal the lid tightly and shake well, until the vinaigrette is
emulsified.

In a small bowl, dress the romaine greens with the vinaigrette and season with salt and pepper.
In a separate bowl, combine the capers and crème fraiche. Spoon 2 teaspoons of the caper/
crème fraiche mixture into each baked phyllo cup. Place a small amount of the dressed romaine
greens into the cups and top with the crumbled smoked salmon.

pair with moshin vineyards russian river valley pinot noir

Murphy-Goode

20 matheson street
healdsburg, ca 95448
707-431-7644

www.murphygoodewinery.com

For our sliders, we cook Snake River Farms pork belly low and slow, then top the meat with house-made Zinfandel sauce. It may be a small sandwich, but the flavor is big.

Makes 36 mini-sandwiches

pork belly sliders

with zinfandel barbecue sauce

ingredients

Zinfandel Barbecue Sauce

1 cup Murphy-Goode Zinfandel
1 cup bottled hoisin sauce
1 cup bottled barbecue sauce

Sliders

1 ounce dried tea leaves (we use Lipton's)
½ gallon water
1 cup kosher salt
2 cups granulated sugar
½ gallon ice
4 pounds pork belly
36 mini hamburger buns

directions brine the pork 1 day in advance

To prepare the sauce, place the Zinfandel in a sauce pot and cook over medium-high heat. Once the wine has reduced by half, add the hoisin and barbeque sauces. Bring the mixture to a boil, then remove from the heat. Refrigerate until ready to use.

To prepare the sliders, wrap the tea leaves in cheesecloth and secure with butcher's twine. In a large pot, combine the water, tea leaf sachet, salt and sugar. Bring the mixture to a boil, remove from the heat, and let steep for 1 hour. Remove the tea sachet and transfer the liquid to a non-reactive container, and add the ice. Cool the brine to below 40°. Add the pork and let it rest in the brine for at least 24 hours, or as long as 48 hours, in the refrigerator.

Preheat the oven to 375°. Remove the pork from the brine and pat it dry with paper towels. Place the pork in a high-sided roasting pan and cook for 2 hours, or until tender. Chill the pork in the refrigerator, then slice it into small medallions.

To serve, crisp the pork in a non-stick sauté pan over medium heat, approximately 1 minute on each side. Steam the buns, and assemble each sandwich with 2 pieces of pork and 1 teaspoon of barbecue sauce.

pair with murphy-goode zinfandel

Pedroncelli Winery

1220 canyon road
geyserville, ca 95441
707-857-3531

www.pedroncelli.com

This tart, similar to those served in northern France, is perfect at any time of day and year. Served hot, cold or anywhere in between, it goes great with a glass or two of Sauvignon Blanc.

Serves 8

leek & goat cheese

tarte flamiche

with apple-endive salad

chef Brian Anderson, Bistro 29

ingredients

Tart Dough
½ pound butter
2 cups flour
pinch of salt
¼ cup cold water

Filling
1 pound leeks, white parts only, thinly sliced
2 tablespoons butter
1 egg
2 egg yolks
½ cup cream
½ cup Gruyere, shredded
½ cup fresh goat cheese

Salad
2 tablespoons sherry vinegar
6 tablespoons olive oil
1 teaspoon fresh tarragon, chopped
salt and pepper, to taste
1 Granny Smith apple, thinly sliced
1 head Belgian endive, cut into 1-inch pieces

directions

To prepare the tart dough, in the bowl of a food processor, combine the butter with 1 cup of the flour and the salt, and process until just combined. Add the remaining cup of flour to the bowl and, with the machine running, add the cold water. Process until the dough comes together, remove it from the bowl, and refrigerate until needed.

To prepare the filling, put the leeks in a pot, cover with water and season with salt. Bring the water to a boil and simmer the leeks for 5 minutes. Drain and return them to the pot, along with the butter. Cook over medium heat until the leeks are tender and dry of any extra liquid. Combine the egg, egg yolks, cream and the 2 cheeses in the pot with the leeks.

Apply non-stick spray to a tart mold. Roll out the dough to ⅛-inch thick and place in the mold. Pour in the filling and bake in a 350° oven for 30 minutes, or until the top is firm and golden brown. Let stand for 15 minutes before serving.

Meanwhile, prepare the salad by mixing the vinegar, oil, tarragon, salt and pepper in a bowl. Toss the apples and endive pieces with the vinaigrette and serve alongside the tart.

pair with pedroncelli sauvignon blanc

Sapphire Hill Winery

55 front street
healdsburg, ca 95448
707-431-1888

www.sapphirehill.com

This wonderfully savory appetizer matches beautifully with our Russian River Valley Estate Pinot Noir. Larger portions of this dish can be served as an entrée; couscous or polenta would complement the flavors of the pork perfectly.

Serves 10

grilled pork tenderloin
with sweet chutney

chef Jeff Anderson

ingredients

4 cups Sapphire Hill Pinot Noir
1 cup Dijon mustard
1-½ pounds pork tenderloin
1 cup dried cherries
1 cup dried cranberries
2 Fuji apples
2 baguettes
olive oil, for brushing

directions

To prepare the marinade, in a mixing bowl, combine 2 cups of the Pinot Noir and the Dijon mustard, and whisk together. Place the tenderloin in a 1-gallon zip lock bag and add the marinade to the bag. Press out as much of the air as you can and seal the bag. Marinate the pork in the refrigerator for 1to 3 hours.

To prepare the chutney, in a saucepan, combine the remaining 2 cups of wine and the dried cherries and berries. Bring the mixture a boil, then reduce the heat and simmer for 5 minutes. Remove the fruit and set it aside, then continue to reduce the wine by half.

Meanwhile, dice the apples into ¼-inch dice. Dice the dehydrated cherries and cranberries and add them back to the wine reduction with the apples, and continue to simmer and reduce for 5 to 7 minutes. Remove from the heat and cover.

Preheat the oven to 350°. Slice the baguettes into ½-inch slices and spread them out on a baking sheet. Brush the bread with olive oil and lightly season with salt and pepper. Toast the baguettes to light golden brown and set aside.

To grill the tenderloin, heat a gas grill to medium-high or prepare a medium-hot charcoal fire. Grill the pork to the desired doneness. Remove it from the grill and let it rest on a cutting board for 10 minutes. Slice the tenderloin into ¼-inch slices.

To serve, place a slice of tenderloin on a toasted baguette slice and add a spoonful of the sweet chutney on top.

pair with sapphire hill estate russian river valley pinot noir

Silver Oak Cellars, Alexander Valley

24625 chianti road
geyserville, ca 95441
707-942-7082

www.silveroak.com

This recipe started with our director of winemaking, Daniel Baron. When he worked in the cellars of Chateau Petrus in Bordeaux, this dish was made to celebrate the last day of pressing. Grilled rib-eye steaks are sliced and served on a baguette, smothered with shallots, red wine and demi-glace. At the end of every harvest, Daniel prepares the dish for Silver Oak employees, often using Cabernet Sauvignon from the last pressed tank of that year's harvest.

Serves 4-6

entrecote

a la cabernet nouveau

chef Dominic Orsini

ingredients

1 clove garlic, chopped
1 teaspoon Dijon mustard
1 tablespoon fresh rosemary, chopped
½ cup olive oil
1 teaspoon salt
4 rib-eye steaks, each 10 ounces
4 ounces butter
8 cups shallots, sliced
2 cups Cabernet Sauvignon
1 bay leaf
8 cups veal stock (not broth)
salt and pepper, to taste
1 baguette

directions

In a 1-gallon zip-lock bag, place the garlic, mustard, rosemary, olive oil and salt. Seal the bag and mix together thoroughly by shaking. Open the bag, add the steaks, and reseal the bag, expelling as much air as possible. Let the steaks marinate at least 1 hour, preferably overnight, in the refrigerator.

Place a 1-gallon sauce pot over medium-high heat and add the butter. After the butter melts, it will start to brown; stir thoroughly until all of the butter is brown, and add the shallots. Stirring occasionally, let the shallots cook until they begin to brown.

Once the shallots are evenly brown, add the wine and bay leaf. Bring the mixture to a boil, and simmer until 95% of the liquid has evaporated. Add the veal stock and bring back to a boil, then simmer until 75% of the liquid has evaporated.

Preheat a grill, and cook the steaks to your desired doneness, sprinkling them with salt and pepper. Let the steaks rest on a cutting board for 10 minutes.

To serve, cut the baguette down the middle so as to open like a sandwich. Slice the steaks into thin ribbons, and pile them down the middle of the baguette. Pour the shallot sauce on top, then slice the baguette into small sandwiches.

pair with silver oak alexander valley cabernet sauvignon

Stephen & Walker Winery

243 healdsburg avenue
healdsburg, ca 95448
707-431-8749

www.trustwine.com

Fried cheese is something my husband, Tony, created in our kitchen when our two sons were small. They would eat just about anything, and Tony found that they especially liked this treat, lured by its intoxicating aroma. Canned cannellini beans can be used instead of dried beans if you want to eliminate the soaking and cooking process.

Makes 24 cups

fried cheese cups

with heirloom tomatoes & white beans

chef Nancy Walker

ingredients

2 cups olive oil
3 garlic cloves, chopped
2 teaspoons rosemary
6 fresh heirloom tomatoes, chopped
4 cups cannellini beans, drained
salt and pepper, to taste
1 cup basil, chopped
1 pound shredded cheese blend

directions

In a sauté pan, heat the olive oil and add the garlic and rosemary. Stir to combine, turn off the heat, and let the herbs and garlic sit for 20 minutes. Strain off the herbs and transfer the infused oil to a glass jar with a lid. Keep refrigerated until ready to use.

In a large bowl, combine the tomatoes, infused oil, beans, salt and pepper. Stir gently to mix and warm, but don't let the beans get mushy. Stir in the basil with about 1 minute of cooking remaining.

Divide the shredded cheese into 24 servings. In a frying pan over medium heat, add the small mounds of cheese (as many as will comfortably fit while remaining separate). Cook until each cheese "pancake" is soft and light golden, about 2 minutes on each side. Be careful not to let the cheese burn.

Remove the cheese "pancakes" from the pan and allow them to cool, draped over small cups. The cheese will harden and will hold its cup shape. Fill each cup with a small spoonful of tomato and bean mixture, and serve.

pair with stephen & walker pinot noir

Taft Street Winery

2030 barlow lane
sebastopol, ca 95472
707-823-2049

www.taftstreetwinery.com

This recipe has been a longtime favorite at Taft Street. We most recently served it at our Founder's Day party, where we found that a slice of salmon + crostini + a glass of Taft Street Chardonnay = heaven!

Serves 10-12

tequila-cured
cold smoked salmon

chef Mike Tierney

ingredients

1-½ cups kosher salt
3 cups brown sugar
1 bunch cilantro leaves, chopped
3 tablespoons ground black pepper
1 salmon fillet, 2½ pounds, skin on
1-½ cups tequila

directions cure the salmon 3 days in advance

In a large bowl, mix together the salt, sugar, cilantro and pepper. Spread ⅓ of the mixture on the bottom on a non-metallic container that is a bit bigger that the salmon fillet.

Remove any bones from the salmon, and lay the fillet skin-side-down on the top of the salt mixture. Pour the tequila over the salmon and cover the fish with the remaining salt mixture. Cover and refrigerate for 3 days.

When you're ready to cook, remove the salmon from the refrigerator and lift it out of its salt shell. Put hardwood in a smoker and ignite. When plenty of smoke is being produced, turn off the smoker and place the salmon in the box, along with a tin of ice. Cold-smoke for 30 to 60 minutes and serve.

pair with taft street russian river valley chardonnay

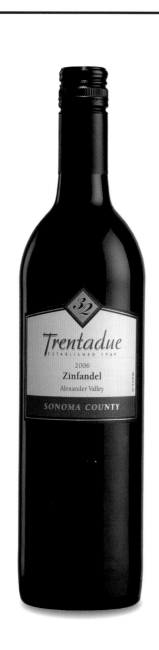

Trentadue Winery

19170 geyserville avenue
geyserville, ca 95441
707-433-3104

www.trentadue.com

Whenever possible, we go to local ranchers and farmers for the various ingredients for our dishes. Northern Sonoma has a wealth of artisan food producers, and this recipe is most authentic if you use local Sonoma lamb and olive oil – and Trentadue Zinfandel, of course.

Serves 8

lamb kabobs

with crimini mushrooms & zinfandel caramelized onions

chef Royalene Mancini

ingredients
bamboo skewers
2 onions, thinly sliced
1 cup Zinfandel
2 pounds of lamb, cut into 1-inch cubes
1 tablespoon cumin
1 tablespoon chili paste
1 tablespoon thyme
salt and pepper, to taste
¼ pound medium crimini mushrooms, sliced
3 tablespoons olive oil

directions soak the skewers for at least 2 hours in water

To prepare the onions, add a splash of olive oil to a sauté pan and cook the onions over medium heat until they're caramelized. Add the Zinfandel and continue to cook until the wine is reduced to nearly dry. Set the onions aside to cool.

Preheat a grill. Season the lamb with the cumin, chili paste, thyme and salt. Season the mushrooms with salt and pepper, and keep the meat and mushrooms separate. On the skewers, alternate the lamb cubes and mushrooms, brush them with olive oil, and grill to the preferred doneness. Top with the onion mixture and enjoy.

pair with trentadue zinfandel

Trione Vineyards & Winery

19550 geyserville avenue
geyserville, ca 95441
707-814-8100

www.trionewinery.com

Frutura Dulce has been served in the
Trione family for decades, particularly during
the holidays. It's a family tradition that has
been passed down for generations.
This dish can be served as vegetarian
by omitting the prosciutto.

Serves 12

trione family

frutura dulce

chef Tim Vallery, Peloton Catering

ingredients

Polenta
1 quart whole milk
1 lemon, zested
1 cup sugar
1 teaspoon almond extract
½ teaspoon vanilla extract
1 cup polenta
4 egg yolks
½ teaspoon kosher salt

Breading
2 cups panko bread crumbs
2 eggs, whisked
3 tablespoons water
1 tablespoon unsalted butter

Crispy Prosciutto
6 slices prosciutto

Goat Cheese Mousse
6 ounces heavy whipping cream
2 garlic cloves, peeled and crushed
2 tablespoons fresh tarragon, chiffonade
kosher salt, to taste
8 ounces Laura Chenel Chevre
2 ounces crème fraiche

directions prepare the polenta 1 day ahead

In a saucepan, heat the milk, lemon, sugar, almond and vanilla extract for 10 minutes. When the milk comes to a simmer, whisk in the polenta. Constantly stir the mixture until the liquid is completely incorporated and the polenta has a smooth consistency. Depending on the type of polenta you use, it should take approximately 20 minutes. Remove the mixture from the heat.

In a mixing bowl, lightly beat the eggs. Pour a small amount of hot polenta into the eggs to heat them evenly, stirring quickly, then add all the eggs to the remaining hot mixture. Spread the polenta in an oiled dish and refrigerate overnight.

In the morning, cut the polenta into serving-size pieces (diamond, round or square shapes). To prepare the breading, add the water to the whisked eggs, and place this mixture in a shallow dish. Place the panko in another shallow dish. Dip each polenta piece into the egg/water mixture, then the bread crumbs. Let the polenta rest in the refrigerator for 45 minutes, or until the pieces become firm. Then sauté them in unsalted butter until they're golden brown on both sides.

To prepare the crispy prosciutto, preheat the oven to 350°. Place the prosciutto slices on a parchment paper-lined baking sheet, and bake for 10 to 15 minutes, or until the prosciutto is crispy. Remove from the oven and allow to cool.

To prepare the goat cheese mousse, in a sauce pot over medium heat, combine the cream, salt, garlic and tarragon. Bring the mixture to a simmer for about 5 minutes, and let it rest for another 15 minutes. Over a double boiler, heat the goat cheese in a stainless steel bowl. Add the cream mixture, and whisk until it is completely smooth. Let the mixture cool for 15 minutes, then fold in the crème fraiche and refrigerate until ready to serve.

To serve, cut the prosciutto slices in half. Place 1 prosciutto piece on a polenta piece and top with a dollop of goat cheese mousse.

pair with trione russian river valley chardonnay

Truett Hurst
Winery

5610 dry creek road
healdsburg, ca 95448
707-433-9545

www.truetthurst.com

This is a new recipe that I developed especially for "A Wine & Food Affair." I was inspired by the spicy, rich flavors of the wines of Dry Creek Valley. The sauce on these bite-size sliders is fresh and light, and the three varieties of ground meat make the meatballs burst with myriad flavors.

Serves 30

spicy meatball sliders

chef Sylvia Hurst

ingredients

Sauce
1 20-ounce can whole peeled tomatoes
1 cup roasted red peppers
2 tablespoons olive oil
1 medium white onion, chopped
4 cloves garlic, minced
1 6-ounce can tomato paste
½ cup Truett Hurst Red Rooster Zinfandel
1 teaspoon red pepper flakes
salt and pepper, to taste

Meatballs
⅓ pound each of ground beef, pork and chicken
⅓ cup breadcrumbs
1 egg, whisked
¼ cup parsley, chopped
⅛ cup green onion, chopped
2 tablespoons Worcestershire sauce
salt and pepper, to taste
30 potato dinner rolls or slider rolls

directions

To prepare the sauce, in a food processor, pulse the tomatoes and red peppers until they're slightly chunky. In a 4-quart pot, heat the olive oil and sauté the onions and garlic for approximately 5 minutes, or until they're translucent. Add the Zinfandel and simmer on low an additional 5 minutes.

Add the tomato/red pepper sauce and the tomato paste to the pot, sprinkle with the red pepper flakes and season with salt and pepper. Simmer the sauce while you make the meatballs.

To prepare the meatballs, combine all the ingredients (minus the rolls) in a large bowl and mix thoroughly with your hands. Roll meatballs into the size of a walnut, and gently drop each one into the tomato sauce as you make them. Simmer for 20 minutes.

To serve, toast the rolls and place a meatball with sauce on each one. Serve immediately.

pair with truett hurst red rooster zinfandel

Vintage Wine Estates

308-b center street
healdsburg, ca 95448
707-921-2893

www.vintagewineestates.com

Meaty, sweet Dungeness crab is a signature Sonoma County ingredient, and so are the crab cakes from Oakville Grocery, which opened on the Healdsburg plaza in 1997. You can substitute with other species of crab, but Pacific Dungeness are large and yield more succulent flesh than most other crabs. Be sure to use Japanese panko bread crumbs.

Makes 50 cakes

oakville grocery signature
crab cakes

ingredients

8 pounds crab meat
2-½ pounds Oakville Mix (green bell pepper, red bell pepper, red onion), finely diced
3 cups mayonnaise
1 cup mustard
2-½ tablespoons garlic, minced
1-½ tablespoons lemon juice
1 teaspoon cayenne
½ bunch thyme, chopped
salt and pepper, to taste
1 pound flour
12 eggs, beaten
1 pound panko bread crumbs
1 bunch parsley, chopped
canola oil, for frying

directions

In a large bowl, blend the crab, vegetables, mayonnaise, mustard, garlic, lemon juice, cayenne, thyme, salt and pepper. Scoop the mixture into 3-ounce balls, and press them gently into patties.

In a large skillet, add canola oil to ¼-inch-depth and heat on high, until the oil has a fine sheen.

Place the flour, beaten eggs, panko and parsley in separate wide, shallow baking dishes. In order, dredge each crab cake in the flour, eggs, bread crumbs and parsley on both sides, and carefully place them in the hot oil. Work in batches so that you don't crowd the pan. Fry the cakes until they're golden brown, approximately 2 to 3 minutes per side, and remove them to paper towels to drain for a minute or two.

Serve the cakes with your favorite remoulade, aioli or tartar sauce. They also make great sandwiches.

pair with sonoma coast vineyards chardonnay or windsor sonoma pinot noir

soups

Amista Vineyards

3320 dry creek road
healdsburg, ca 95448
707-431-9200

www.amistavineyards.com

Mike Farrow, our winemaker, proprietor and home chef, first tried his hand at cassoulet one chilly autumn evening and it's been a favorite of ours ever since – rich, hearty and satisfying – like a wonderful friendship. Chef John Franchetti presents a variation on this popular dish in soup form. Begin preparing the dish two days before you plan to serve it. The duck confit legs are available in most gourmet markets.

Serves 10-12

cassoulet amista

chef John Franchetti, Rosso Pizzeria & Wine Bar

ingredients

2 pounds white beans
5 tablespoons extra virgin olive oil
2 medium onions, cubed
3 carrots, sliced into rounds
12 cloves of garlic, peeled and roughly chopped
6 ounces prosciutto, in 1 piece, then cubed
8 ounces pancetta, in 1 piece, then cubed
1 tomato, peeled and chopped
5 quarts chicken stock

1 herb bouquet (4 sprigs parsley, 2 sprigs thyme, 1 bay leaf and 3 small ribs celery, tied together)
6 duck confit legs
1 pound garlic sausage
2 tablespoons breadcrumbs
4 tablespoons parsley, finely chopped
4 tablespoons lemon zest
3 tablespoons walnut oil
salt and pepper, to taste

directions begin this dish 2 days in advance

Rinse the beans under cool running water. Cover with water and soak overnight.

The next day, in a large pan, sauté the onions, carrots and garlic in the olive oil until they're soft. Add salt and pepper to taste. Add the prosciutto and pancetta and cook an additional minute or so. Add the tomato, 2 quarts of the stock and the herb bouquet. Drain the beans and add them to the pan. Bring the mixture to a simmer and cook for 1-½ hours, or until the beans are tender. Remove them from the heat, let cool, cover, and refrigerate overnight.

The following day, remove any fat from the top of the bean mixture. Add the remaining 3 quarts of stock and warm the pan on low heat. Add the duck confit legs and garlic sausage, and simmer for 1 hour; add salt and pepper if needed.

After 1 hour, pull the duck legs out, remove the meat from the bone, and chop the meat. Remove the sausage, chop it into ½-inch pieces, and return the sausage and duck to the pot. Remove and discard the herb bouquet. In a small bowl, mix the bread crumbs, parsley and lemon zest.

To serve, ladle the cassoulet into a large bowl. Garnish with the bread crumb mixture and walnut oil, then sprinkle with salt and pepper.

pair with amista morningsong vineyards dry creek valley syrah

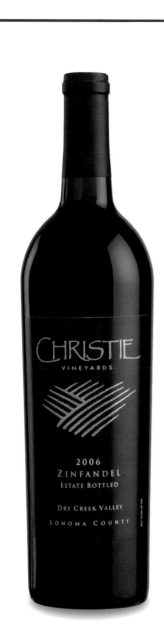

Christie Estate Winery & Vineyards

54 front street
healdsburg, ca 95448
707-433-3097

www.christievineyards.com

Pumpkin is an American food classic, particularly during the holidays, yet it's also a key ingredient in Asian cuisine. This soup has an Asian spiciness that pairs beautifully with our Dry Creek Valley Zinfandel. Be sure to use sweet cooking pumpkins, and not the bland ones that are carved for Halloween.

Serves 8

spiced
pumpkin soup

vegi

ingredients

6 pounds sweet pumpkin
2 cups shallots
2 cups heavy cream
1 gallon vegetable stock
2 tablespoons fresh sage
1 tablespoon chili paste
1 teaspoon Chinese Five Spice
1 cup peanut oil
salt and pepper, to taste

directions preheat oven to 350°

Cut the pumpkins in half, scrape out the seeds, and brush the flesh with a little of the peanut oil. Roast the pumpkins, exposed flesh up, until they're tender and golden brown; the cooking time will depend on the size of the pumpkins. Let the pumpkins cool, then scoop the flesh away from the skin and set the flesh aside.

In a soup pot, roast the shallots until they're caramelized, and roughly chop them. Return the shallots to the pot and add the pumpkin flesh, cream, stock, sage, chili paste, Five Spice and peanut oil. Stir to combine, bring to a boil, and simmer for 15 minutes.

Puree the mixture in a blender, in batches, or use an immersion blender in the soup pot. To serve, ladle the soup into bowls and serve with good-quality local bread.

pair with christie dry creek valley zinfandel

Farmhouse Inn & Restaurant

7871 river road
forestville, ca 95436
707-887-3300

www.farmhouseinn.com

The fall-winter season brings one of Sonoma County's finest food products to market, Dungeness crab. The sea-sweet crab meat in this soup gets a savory, spicy kick from green garlic and espelette pepper (piment d'Espelette, a hot dried pepper from France's Basque region), which adds a sophisticated complexity to asparagus soup.

Serves 4

asparagus soup

with green garlic & chile-roasted Dungeness crab

chef Steve Litke

ingredients

2 tablespoons butter
1 large leek (white and pale green parts only), halved lengthwise and thickly sliced
1 large onion, chopped
2 celery stalks, chopped
1 pound asparagus, ends trimmed, spears coarsely chopped (reserve some tips for garnish)
4 cups vegetable stock

2 cups spinach leaves, chopped
1 bunch green garlic, finely chopped
4 tablespoons olive oil
½ pound butter
3 tablespoons espelette pepper
½ cup Dungeness crab leg meat
salt and pepper, to taste

directions

Melt the butter in a large, heavy saucepan over medium heat. Add the leek, onion and celery and sauté until they're soft, about 5 minutes.

Add the stock and bring the mixture to a boil. Reduce the heat and simmer for 5 minutes. Add the asparagus and simmer until the asparagus is tender, 5 to 7 minutes.

Take the pan off the heat and add the spinach. Cover the pan and allow the spinach to wilt, about 3 minutes.

Working in batches, puree the soup in a blender until smooth. Season with salt and pepper. Strain the soup into a bowl over an ice bath, to cool it quickly and preserve its color. Cover and chill the bowl in the refrigerator, up to 1 day ahead.

Preheat the oven to 400°.

Sauté the green garlic in the oil until it's soft. Set it aside and let it cool. In a medium bowl, beat the butter and pepper together, and fold in the green garlic, asparagus tips and crab. Spoon the mixture into an oven-proof dish and roast in the oven for 3 to 4 minutes, until the butter is melted and the crab is hot.

To serve, slowly re-warm the soup to a simmer but do not let it boil. Place ¼ of the crab mixture in the center of 4 soup bowls. Ladle the soup around each crab mound, and serve immediately.

pair with your favorite sonoma county sauvignon blanc

Forchini Vineyards & Winery

5141 dry creek road
healdsburg, ca 95448
707-431-8886

www.forchini.com

Autumn comes with crisp mornings and longer evenings that begin with a wood fire. Nothing is better for the season than good soup for dinner. This quick and easy corn chowder can be started when the fire is lit. Open a bottle of Forchini wine, pour a glass for the cook, and enjoy this yummy soup with local breads and cheeses.

Serves 4

autumn
corn chowder

chef Randi Kauppi, Oui Cater

ingredients

4 tablespoons olive oil
2 tablespoons celery, finely diced
1 small carrot, finely diced
2 jalapeno peppers, seeded and thinly sliced
1 onion, finely diced
1 10-ounce package frozen white corn kernels
1 large potato, peeled and diced
1 cup water or vegetable broth
½ teaspoon salt
¼ teaspoon pepper
2 cups half-and-half
2 tablespoons flour
¼ teaspoon paprika
2 tablespoons parsley, minced

directions

In a soup pot, heat the oil. Add the celery, carrot, onion and peppers, and cook for 2 minutes. Add the corn, potatoes, water or broth, salt, pepper and paprika. Bring to a boil, lower the heat to medium, and simmer, covered, for 10 minutes, or until the potatoes are tender.

Whisk ½ cup of the half-and-half with the flour. Add it gradually to the pot, along with the remaining half-and-half. Cook, stirring, until the soup comes to a boil and thickens.

To serve, ladle the chowder into bowls and garnish with the parsley.

pair with forchini papa nonno tuscan style red, russian river valley chardonnay or dry creek valley zinfandel

Graton Ridge Cellars

3561 gravenstein highway north
sebastopol, ca 95472
707-823-3040

www.gratonridge.com

This recipe has been handed down over the years by Barbara Paul's family, and the soup is wonderful on a cold day or evening. Try adding diced zucchini and other vegetables in your pantry, so that it has a slightly different taste each time you make it.

Serves 8-10

grandma rosie's

minestrone soup

chef Barbara Paul

ingredients

16 cups chicken stock (homemade or Swanson's)
6 potatoes, peeled and diced
4 medium carrots, diced
2 medium onions, chopped
½ small head of cabbage, chopped
1-½ cups spinach or chard, chopped
½ cup dried split peas
1 16-ounce can whole tomatoes, with juice
2 tablespoons tomato paste
salt and pepper, to taste

directions

In a large stock pot, add the chicken stock and bring to a simmer on the stovetop over medium heat.

Add the remaining ingredients, stir to combine, and simmer very slowly, for 1-½ to 2 hours, stirring occasionally.

When the potatoes and carrots are just tender, remove the pot from the stove and ladle the minestrone into large bowls as a main course. Serve with crusty Italian bread, if desired, to mop up the delicious juices.

pair with graton ridge cellars pinot noir or zinfandel

Hart's Desire Wines

53 front street
healdsburg, ca 95448
707-433-3097

www.hartsdesirewines.com

This recipe was inspired by too many dreary days in a row last winter. Wanting a hearty soup that would make us feel warm and healthy, we came up with Winter Welcome Chili. We used carrots and parsnips from our garden, and added red bell peppers for color. The adobo and chipotle peppers warm us inside and out.

Serves 4

winter welcome chili

chef Garrett Adair

ingredients

¼ cup vegetable oil
1 yellow onion, chopped
2 garlic cloves, finely chopped
1 red bell pepper, cut into ½-inch pieces
½ pound parsnips, cut into ½-inch pieces
½ pound carrots, cut into ½-inch pieces
1 tablespoon ground cumin
1 teaspoon salt
1 14-ounce can peeled Italian tomatoes

1 chipotle pepper in adobo (canned), plus 1 tablespoon adobo sauce
1-½ cups water
1 large can red kidney beans, drained
salt and pepper, to taste
1 red onion, chopped
¼ cup cilantro, chopped
¼ cup sour cream
tortilla chips

directions

In a heavy enameled cast-iron casserole or Dutch oven, heat the oil. Add the onion and garlic and cook over high heat, stirring, until the vegetables are slightly soft, approximately 3 minutes.

Add the bell pepper, parsnips and carrots and cook, stirring occasionally, for 5 minutes. Add the cumin and salt, stir, and cook for 1 minute.

In a blender, puree the tomatoes and their juices with the chipotle pepper, adobo sauce and water, until very smooth. Add the puree and kidney beans to the casserole and bring to a boil. Partially cover the casserole and simmer the chili over moderate heat, until the vegetables are tender, about 20 minutes.

Season to taste with salt and pepper. Top with the red onion, cilantro and sour cream, and serve with tortilla chips.

pair with hart's desire russian river valley petite sirah

Mazzocco
Sonoma Winery

1400 lytton springs road
healdsburg, ca 95448
707-431-8159

www.mazzocco.com

Here is a local twist on the classic "broccoli with cheese" dish, in soup form. First-of-the-season broccoli is pureed with butter, onions and creamy blue cheese to form a surprisingly simple-to-prepare soup that is a perfect pairing with Zinfandel. This recipe also works well with cauliflower.

Serves 4

broccoli soup

with point reyes original blue cheese & toasted almonds

vegi

ingredients

1 head broccoli (about 1-½ pounds)
2 tablespoons unsalted butter
1 yellow onion, peeled and diced
1 tablespoon flour
3 cups vegetable stock
4 ounces Point Reyes Original Blue Cheese
salt and pepper, to taste
1 tablespoon almonds, toasted and finely chopped

directions

Clean and trim the broccoli, removing any little wiry leaves. Separate the florets from the stalk. Using a peeler or paring knife, remove the toughest part of the stalk, so that only the tender heart remains. Cut the florets and stalks into 1-inch pieces, keeping them separate.

In a soup pot over medium heat, melt the butter, add the onion and broccoli stalk pieces, and cook until the vegetables are soft but not browned. Add the flour and stir to coat the vegetables. Cook for 2 minutes but do not brown, turning down the heat, if necessary.

Add the stock to the pot and bring to a boil. Simmer the soup for 30 minutes, then return it to a boil and add the broccoli florets. Cook for 5 minutes, then remove the pot from the heat. Working in batches, carefully ladle the soup into a blender and puree (be careful not to overload the blender). Add the cheese to the soup in small increments while the blender runs. Alternatively, use an immersion blender and puree the soup in the pot. Add salt and pepper, if necessary.

To serve, ladle the soup into warm bowls, top with the almonds and serve immediately.

pair with your favorite mazzocco zinfandel

Papapietro Perry Winery

4791 dry creek road
healdsburg, ca 95448
707-433-0422

www.papapietro-perry.com

The flavors of mushroom and thyme work well with many different wines, especially our Pinot Noirs. You can make this soup a day in advance, so the flavors can come together. This is a vegetarian dish if you use vegetable stock; chicken stock works just as well for those who eat meat.

Serves 4

wild
mushroom soup

chefs Bruce Riezenman and Steven Taub, Park Avenue Catering

ingredients

2 tablespoons butter
1 tablespoon garlic, chopped
1 large onion, finely diced
1 large carrot, thinly sliced
salt and pepper, to taste
1 pound wild mushrooms
1 pound domestic mushrooms
2 ounces dried porcini mushrooms
1 tablespoon fresh thyme, chopped
1 large bay leaf
1-½ quarts vegetable stock (or chicken stock)
1 cup heavy cream

directions

In a saucepan over medium heat, place the butter, garlic, onion and carrot. Add salt and pepper to taste. Cover and "sweat" the vegetables until they're cooked.

Add the mushrooms (both fresh and dried), thyme and bay leaf. Cover and cook for 10 minutes.

Add the stock and cream, and simmer for a few minutes. Add salt and/or pepper, if necessary, and continue to simmer for 1/2 hour. Let the soup cool, puree it in a blender, then adjust the seasonings one last time before serving.

pair with papapietro perry pinot noir

Ridge Vineyards Lytton Springs

650 lytton springs road
healdsburg, ca 95448
707-433-7721

www.ridgewine.com

This soup is perfect for when the weather in Dry Creek Valley becomes chilly, the leaves in the vineyards turn red and gold, and our new wines are released. We love to use the new crop of cannellini beans, which are creamy and melt in your mouth. Duck confit legs can be purchased at most gourmet markets.

Serves 6-8

cannellini bean soup
with duck confit

ingredients

1 pound cannellini beans
(we love Phipps Ranch Italian Butter Beans)
4 duck confit legs, room temperature
4 tablespoons olive oil
2 medium yellow onions, finely diced
2 large carrots, finely diced
2 celery stalks, finely diced
6 large garlic cloves, finely minced
2 bay leaves

2 large thyme sprigs
2 whole cloves
6 cups chicken stock
8 cups water
1 15-ounce can diced tomatoes, drained
salt and pepper
½ cup Cognac
½ cup Italian parsley, minced

directions soak the beans 1 day ahead

Cover the beans in cold water by 1 inch, and allow to soak, chilled, overnight. Drain the beans and discard the liquid.

The next day, remove the skin and bones from the duck legs, reserving both, and coarsely shred the meat.

In a large, heavy pot, heat the oil over medium heat until it shimmers, then cook the reserved bones, onions, carrots, celery, garlic, bay leaves, thyme and cloves, stirring occasionally, until the vegetables are softened, about 8 minutes.

Add the drained beans, broth, water and tomatoes and simmer, partially covered, stirring and skimming the foam occasionally, until the beans are tender, about 50 minutes.

Meanwhile, thinly slice the reserved duck skin, then lightly season it with salt and pepper. Cook the skin over low heat in a dry, nonstick skillet, stirring to separate, until the fat is rendered and the skin is crisp, 6 to 8 minutes.

Discard the bay leaves, bones and thyme from the soup. Transfer 2 cups of the solids and 1 cup of the liquid from the soup to a blender and blend until smooth, then return the puree to the soup pot. Stir in 2 teaspoons of salt and 1/2 teaspoon of pepper and keep warm, covered.

Heat the Cognac in a small saucepan over low heat just until warm, then ignite the brandy with a long kitchen match (use caution, as flames will shoot up). When the flames subside, stir the Cognac into the soup, along with the meat, parsley, and salt and pepper to taste. Sprinkle with crispy skin, and serve.

pair with ridge lytton springs zinfandel blend

Rodney Strong Vineyards

11455 old redwood highway
healdsburg, ca 95448
707-431-1533

www.rodneystrong.com

We are never shy about telling tasting room visitors about this delicious soup from Zin restaurant, especially when we can pair it with one of our wines. Each time we eat this soup at the winery, we tell Zin chefs Jeff and Susan Mall to prepare 20 portions more than we need, so we can all have seconds.

Serves 6-8

butternut
squash & apple soup
with lemon cream & crispy sage

chefs Jeff and Susan Mall, Zin Restaurant & Wine Bar

ingredients

Lemon Cream
½ cup crème fraîche
½ teaspoon lemon zest, grated
1-½ tablespoons fresh lemon juice
salt and freshly ground pepper, to taste

Crispy Sage Leaves
2 tablespoons unsalted butter
10 fresh sage leaves
salt for sprinkling

Soup
1 stick unsalted butter
1 butternut squash (about 2 pounds),
peeled, seeded and cubed
1 yellow onion, chopped
2 green apples, peeled, cored and
chopped
6 fresh sage leaves
4 cups chicken stock or broth
½ teaspoon organic apple cider vinegar
(preferably Nana Mae's)
1 tablespoon kosher salt
½ cup heavy cream

directions

To prepare the lemon cream, combine all the ingredients in a small bowl and stir until blended. Set aside.

To prepare the crispy sage leaves, melt the butter in a saucepan over medium heat, until it foams. Add the sage leaves and sauté until they're crisp, 45 seconds to 1 minute. Using a slotted spoon, transfer the leaves to paper towels to drain. Sprinkle the leaves lightly with salt, and break them into smaller pieces. Set aside.

To prepare the soup, in a large pot, melt the butter over medium-high heat until it turns a light brown. Stir in the squash, onion, apples and fresh sage leaves. Cook, stirring often, until the vegetables and apples are golden brown, about 10 minutes.

Stir in the stock or broth, vinegar and salt, and bring to a boil. Reduce the heat to a simmer and cook until the squash is tender when pierced, about 15 minutes. Stir in the cream. Working in batches, puree the soup in a blender until smooth. Return to the soup pot and keep warm.

Ladle the hot soup into shallow bowls. Top each bowl with a dollop of lemon cream and a sprinkling of sage leaves, and serve immediately.

pair with rodney strong charlotte's home sauvignon blanc

Selby Winery

215 center street
healdsburg, ca 95448
707-431-1288

www.selbywinery.com

Is there any ingredient more decadent than lobster? For this soup, chef Sean Thompson uses a lobster base that can be purchased in gourmet grocery stores and online (try Amazon.com). The base provides a concentrated lobster flavor to this bisque, which Sean recommends serving in a sourdough bread bowl from Costeaux Bakery in Healdsburg.

Serves 8-10

sean's famous
lobster bisque

chef Sean Thompson

ingredients

4 ounces lobster base
1 cup tomato paste
5 cups hot water
1 tablespoon fresh thyme
1 tablespoon fresh tarragon
1 tablespoon ground white pepper
2 tablespoons shallots, finely chopped
1 cup Selby Russian River Valley Pinot Noir
¾ cup butter
1 cup all-purpose flour
1-½ cups cooked bay shrimp
2 quarts heavy cream

directions

Dissolve the lobster base and tomato paste in the hot water. Put the mixture into a large stock pot, add the thyme, tarragon, white pepper, shallots and Pinot Noir, and bring to a boil.

Mix together a light roux of the butter and flour. Whisk the roux into the boiling soup and continue whisking until the bisque has thickened.

Place the cooked bay shrimp into a food processor and process until smooth. Add the shrimp to the hot soup, and stir in the heavy cream. Serve immediately.

pair with selby russian river valley pinot noir or chardonnay

Toad Hollow Vineyards

409-a healdsburg avenue
healdsburg, ca 95448
707-431-8667

www.toadhollow.com

This rich and hearty soup can be made with a variety of mushrooms. Debbie Rickards from our tasting room created this recipe after she received, as a gift, a bountiful box of mixed wild mushrooms and needed to use them right away. You can use any combination of mushrooms, including small criminis and large portobello mushrooms, and if you can find them, hedgehogs, porcinis, oysters and chanterelles. For safety, be sure to use only purchased wild mushrooms from a certified grocery source.

Serves 10-12

deb's "wild"

cream of mushroom soup

chef Debbie Rickards

ingredients

1 pound assorted wild mushrooms
1-½ tablespoons extra virgin olive oil
1 stick plus 1-½ tablespoons sweet butter
1 large onion, chopped,
1 large carrot, diced
2 sprigs fresh thyme
salt and pepper, to taste
3 cups chicken stock
3 cups water

3 leeks, chopped (white and light green parts only)
¼ cup all-purpose flour
1 cup Toad Hollow Chardonnay
1 cup half-and-half
1 cup heavy cream
1-½ teaspoons fresh thyme, minced
fresh chives, minced, for garnish
white truffle oil, for garnish

directions

Clean the mushrooms with dry paper towels. Remove the stems and chop them coarsely. Slice the caps ¼-inch thick, and set aside.

For the mushroom stock, heat and melt together the olive oil and the 1-½ tablespoons of butter in a large stock pot. Add the mushroom stems (not the caps), onion, carrot, thyme sprigs, salt and pepper. Cook over medium-low heat for 15 minutes, until the vegetables are tender.

Add the chicken stock and water and bring the mixture to a boil. Reduce the heat slightly and simmer for 30 minutes, or until the liquid is reduced to 4-½ cups. Strain the stock and set aside. Add more chicken stock or water if the amount of stock is short of the 4-½-cup measure.

Next, melt the stick of butter in the pot, add the leeks, and cook until they are lightly browned, about 15 minutes. Add the sliced mushrooms and continue cooking for 10 minutes. Sprinkle the mixture with the flour, stir, and cook 1 minute more. Add the Chardonnay and stir, making sure to scrape the bottom of the pot to get all the bits of flour.

Add the strained mushroom stock, thyme, salt and pepper. Bring the mixture to a boil, then reduce the heat and simmer for 15 minutes. Add the half-and-half and cream.

To serve, ladle the soup into bowls and garnish with a sprinkle of chives and a few drops of truffle oil.

pair with toad hollow francine's selection chardonnay or goldie's vines pinot noir

Wilson Winery

1960 dry creek road
healdsburg, ca 95448
707-433-4355

www.wilsonwinery.com

The abundance of mushrooms available in
Sonoma County gives us myriad ways to use
them in wine-friendly dishes.
For this soup, we use four savory
mushrooms – three fresh and one dried –
to complement our Zinfandels.

Serves 12

four-mushroom soup

chef Michael Matson, Vintage Valley Catering

ingredients

2 cups shallots
¼ cup garlic cloves
¾ cup olive oil
½ pound salted butter
3 cups shiitake mushrooms, chopped
3 cups crimini mushrooms, chopped
3 cups oyster mushrooms, chopped
1 cup dried porcini mushrooms
2 tablespoons fresh thyme, chopped
2 cups Wilson Zinfandel
1 cup heavy cream
2 bay leaves
1 gallon vegetable stock
2 tablespoons sherry vinegar
2 cups croutons, homemade or purchased

directions preheat oven to 350°

Place the shallots and garlic cloves in a shallow, oven-proof pan, drizzle with the olive oil, and roast them in the oven until they're tender and brown.

In a 2-gallon stock pot, add the butter, mushrooms and the roasted garlic and shallots, with their oil, and heat until the ingredients are combined. Deglaze the pot with the Zinfandel.

Add the remaining ingredients, except for the croutons, and bring them to a boil. Simmer for 30 minutes.

In a blender, puree the soup, and top with the croutons before serving.

pair with your favorite wilson zinfandel

salads & sides

Balletto Vineyards

5700 occidental road
santa rosa, ca 95401
707-568-2455

www.ballettovineyards.com

This recipe is one that I initially created to accompany mashed potatoes. It has become a family favorite for all sorts of occasions and is used on various dishes. The Balletto wine provides an excellent balance to the chicken broth and lends elegance to the sauce.
In addition to potatoes, serve it with poultry, rice, vegetables and more.

Serves 6

chardonnay gravy

chef Helen Sharrocks

ingredients

2 cups chicken broth (homemade or canned)
1/3 cup Balletto Estate Chardonnay
4 tablespoons butter
4 tablespoons flour
salt and pepper, to taste
dried rosemary or thyme (optional)

directions

In a saucepan, heat the chicken broth and wine to almost boiling. In a separate saucepan, melt the butter, then add the flour, and whisk the mixture until it's smooth and aromatic.

Add the flour mixture to the broth and bring to a boil, stirring constantly. Continue to whisk the gravy until it thickens. Add salt and pepper to taste, and if you like, a dash of rosemary or thyme. Stir to combine, remove to a gravy boat, and serve.

pair with balletto estate chardonnay

Fern Grove Cottages

16650 highway 116
guerneville, ca 95446
888-243-2674

www.ferngrove.com

Prior to my innkeeper days, I enjoyed
entertaining in my home garden in Virginia.
This recipe was a big hit – simple yet with
maximum impact. This salad is excellent on
a balmy summer night, and goes perfectly
with a bottle of Pinot Noir.

Serves 4

heavenly
cheese & pear salad

chef Margaret Kennett

ingredients

2 pears
4 tablespoons butter, melted
8 ounces blue cheese, crumbled
salad greens of your choice
4 tablespoons walnut oil
sea salt, to taste

directions preheat the oven to broil

Peel, core and slice the pears, and place them in a foil-lined broiler pan. Brush the pears with melted butter and broil them for approximately 2 minutes.

Remove the pears from the broiler and sprinkle them with the crumbled blue cheese. Return the pears to the oven and broil again, until the cheese is soft and gooey.

Toss the greens with the walnut oil and a dash of sea salt, top with the broiled pears and cheese, and serve immediately.

pair with russian river valley pinot noir

Matrix Winery

3291 westside road
healdsburg, ca 95448
707-433-1911

www.matrixwinery.com

Focaccia is great as sandwich bread, wonderful for dipping into extra-virgin olive oil, and a fine accompaniment with any meal. When topped with such savory ingredients as pesto, roasted red peppers, red onions, goat cheese, herbs, olive spread and sun-dried tomatoes, focaccia can be a meal by itself. Be creative with the toppings. This recipe is from Costeaux French Bakery in Healdsburg.

Serves 8-10

costeaux focaccia

ingredients

2 cups bread flour
¼ teaspoon salt
2 teaspoons olive oil
¾ cup whole milk
1-¼ ounce package fresh active yeast, crumbled
olive oil
coarse sea salt

directions preheat oven to 400°

In a large bowl, combine the first 5 ingredients. Mix together by hand or with an electric mixer fitted with a dough hook, for 8 to 12 minutes, until the mixture is well-combined. Finish by hand, kneading the dough until it's smooth. Transfer the dough to a clean bowl and cover it with plastic wrap or a clean cloth, then place it a warm spot (preferably 75° or higher). Let the dough double in size.

When doubled, remove the dough from the bowl and divide it in half. Place each piece on a sheet pan or pizza stone, and flatten and dimple the dough with your hands and fingers to make approximately 2 10-inch rounds.

Brush the rounds with olive oil and sprinkle them with sea salt. Bake approximately 30 to 40 minutes, until done.

pair with your favorite matrix pinot noir

Medlock Ames
Vintners

3487 alexander valley road
healdsburg, ca 95448
707-431-8845

www.medlockames.com

In our tasting room, we always include food
pairings with our wine flights, and this recipe
allows us to serve a crowd on busy days.
You can find Meyer lemon olive oil in
local gourmet markets; Laura Chenel
goat cheese is widely available.

Serves 4

ratatouille tart

with laura chenel goat cheese

chef Tosha Callahan

ingredients

Filling
2 sprigs each of thyme, sage and tarragon
2 tablespoons Meyer lemon olive oil
1 large onion, chopped
3 cloves garlic, minced
5 ripe tomatoes, skin and seeds removed, diced
vegetable stock, if necessary
4 ounces Laura Chenel goat cheese
1 Meyer lemon, juiced
salt and pepper, to taste
1 baked 10-inch tart shell, homemade or prepared

Grilled Ratatouille Vegetables
1 Japanese eggplant
1 yellow summer squash
1 zucchini squash
1 Roma tomato
Meyer lemon olive oil, for drizzling
salt and pepper, to taste

directions

To prepare the tart filling, place the thyme, sage and tarragon in a "sack" of cheesecloth and tie it with twine.

In a sauté pan over medium heat, warm the Meyer lemon olive oil until it turns glossy and transparent. Add the onion and garlic, and cook until they're slightly soft. Add the herb bundle and the tomatoes, and reduce the heat to low. Simmer the mixture until it's creamy; add vegetable stock, if necessary, to achieve smooth consistency.

Simmer for 1 hour, stirring as the sauce thickens. Set it aside to cool, then fold in the goat cheese, lemon juice and salt and pepper.

To prepare the grilled vegetables, slice the eggplant, squashes and tomato into thin medallions, and sprinkle them with Meyer lemon olive oil, salt and pepper. Grill each medallion on both sides until lightly colored, and set aside.

Fill the tart shell with the goat cheese-tomato mixture and layer the grilled vegetable medallions over the surface. Finish with a last drizzle of lemon olive oil and a sprinkle of salt, and serve.

pair with medlock ames sauvignon blanc

pasta & rice

D'Argenzio Winery

1301 cleveland avenue
santa rosa, ca 95401
707-280-4658

www.dargenziowine.com

In Italy, this dish is called strozzapreti al cinghiale con porcini. Strozzapreti (stroh-tzuh-PRAY-tee) are short, thin pasta shapes available in most Italian gourmet markets. You can substitute with any short, cylindrical pasta, such as gemelli or penne, yet strozzapreti authenticate this Tuscan dish. Wild porcini mushrooms grown in the wet, cool regions of Sonoma County are a winter culinary treat.

Serves 4

short pasta with wild boar

& sonoma county wild porcini mushrooms

chef Rita Faglia, Riviera Ristorante

ingredients

4 tablespoons Tuscan organic olive oil
1 cup white onions, chopped
2 tablespoons celery, chopped
1 tablespoon garlic, chopped
1 medium porcini mushroom, sliced
½ teaspoon dried rosemary
1 teaspoon Italian parsley
1 pound ground wild boar
2 cups peeled tomatoes
salt and pepper, to taste
1 pound (16 ounces) dried strozzapreti pasta

directions

In a large sauté pan, heat the oil and cook the onions, celery and garlic until they're caramelized. Add the porcini and let the mixture simmer until the mushrooms are soft. Add the boar and the herbs, and simmer for 20 minutes.

Add the peeled tomatoes and continue cooking slowly for 40 more minutes, seasoning with salt and pepper, if necessary.

While the sauce is in its last simmering stage, add the pasta to a large pot of boiling salted water, stirring, until it's al dente. Drain the pasta, divide it among 4 plates, and top with the warm boar sauce.

pair with d'argenzio pinor noir

Harvest Moon Estate & Winery

2192 olivet road
santa rosa, ca 95401
707-573-8711

www.harvestmoonwinery.com

This pasta bursts with color, from the use
of green, red, yellow and purple bell peppers
(or any combination you can find).
We use our estate-grown and bottled
olive oil in this dish, yet any high-quality
extra virgin olive oil will be fine.

Serves 6-10

estate grown

pasta primavera

chef Erin Elise Randol

ingredients

1 cup bell peppers, sliced into thin strips
½ cup yellow crookneck squash, sliced into ¼-inch-thick rounds
½ cup heirloom striped zucchini squash, sliced into ¼-inch-thick rounds
½ cup zucchini, sliced into ½-inch-thick rounds
¾ cup broccoli florets
1-½ cups crimini mushrooms, quartered
2 tablespoons extra virgin olive oil
6-8 garlic cloves, minced
sprigs of rosemary, basil and thyme
4 tablespoons basil pesto (homemade or prepared)
splash of Harvest Moon Russian River Valley Zinfandel (optional)
1 cup jarred, marinated artichoke hearts, quartered
1 16-ounce bag tri-color rotini (corkscrew) pasta
parmesan or romano cheese, grated

directions

Slice the peppers and squashes. Separate the broccoli into bite-size florets. Mince the garlic. Quarter the mushrooms and dehydrate them in a dry sauté pan over medium heat, until they've stopped releasing their moisture.

Season the pan with the olive oil. Return the heat to medium, and add the garlic, herbs, pesto and Zinfandel (if using). Then add the peppers, stir, and cover the pan for 1 minute to allow the peppers to soften. Toss in the broccoli, cook for 2 to 3 minutes, then add the squashes and cook another 2 minutes more. Add the artichoke hearts, and simmer the mixture for 5 to 10 minutes.

Meanwhile, in a large pot of boiling water, add a pinch of salt and cook the rotini according to package directions. When the pasta is done, strain it and add it to the vegetable medley. Sprinkle with grated cheese, blend, and serve.

pair with harvest moon russian river valley zinfandel

Kokomo Winery

4791 dry creek road
healdsburg, ca 95448
707-433-0200

www.kokomowines.com

This recipe features fall wild mushrooms, and I like to use chanterelles for their woodsy flavor. Feel free to use whichever mushrooms you can buy on the day you prepare this dish. Marin French Camembert, produced in Petaluma, is my choice of cheese for this dish, which is added just before plating.

Serves 4-6

risotto

with camembert & wild mushrooms

chef Jason Denton, Jackson's Bar & Oven

vegi

ingredients

6 cups mushroom stock (or vegetable stock)
2 tablespoons olive oil
2 yellow onions, finely chopped
3 cloves garlic, minced
2 cups arborio rice
1-½ cups Kokomo Pinot Noir

salt
black pepper
1 pound chanterelles or other wild
mushrooms
1 tablespoon fresh thyme, chopped
8 ounces Marin French Camembert
1 bunch chives, chopped

directions preheat oven to 400°

Heat the stock in a large pot over medium-high heat.

To prepare the risotto, warm 1 tablespoon of the olive oil in a large sauce pot over medium heat. Add the onions and garlic, and sauté until they're tender. Add the rice to the pot and toast it, stirring often with a wooden spoon to keep the onions and garlic from over-browning.

Add 1 cup of the Pinot Noir to deglaze the pot, and cook out the alcohol. Stir the rice constantly, adding approximately 8 ounces of hot stock at a time, as the mixture thickens. Season with salt and pepper as you go, and cook until all the stock has evaporated.

To prepare the mushrooms, cut them into large pieces and place them in a roasting pan. Drizzle the remaining 1 tablespoon of olive oil and the fresh thyme over the mushrooms and season with salt and pepper. Roast in the oven until the moisture evaporates and the mushrooms are brown.

To serve, stir the Camembert into the risotto until it's melted, then add the mushrooms. Stir gently, and spoon the mixture into shallow bowls. Sprinkle with the chopped chives, and enjoy.

pair with kokomo sonoma coast pinot noir

Korbel
Champagne
Cellars

13250 river road
guerneville, ca 95446
707-824-7000

www.korbel.com

This pasta has been a mainstay and
constant favorite in the deli at Korbel for more
than 13 years. The orecchiette – "small ears"
pasta – can be substituted with seashell
pasta. You can use any of the
Korbel champagnes in the dressing.

Serves 10-12

orecchiette pasta

with melon & champagne-cracked peppercorn dressing

chef Robin Lehnhoff-McCray

vegi

ingredients

Dressing
3 egg yolks
2 tablespoons Dijon mustard
1 tablespoon garlic, chopped
3 ounces champagne vinegar
3 ounces Korbel Brut Rosé
1 cup Asiago cheese, grated
1 tablespoon freshly cracked peppercorns
2 teaspoons salt
3 cups olive oil

Pasta
1 pound orecchiette pasta
2 cups celery, chopped
1 cup yellow onion, sliced thin
1 cup Asiago cheese, grated
3 cups cantaloupe melon, diced
½ cup parsley, chopped
salt and pepper, to taste

directions

To prepare the dressing, combine the yolks, mustard, garlic, vinegar and wine in a food processor and mix for 1 minute. Add the Asiago, salt and pepper. Slowly drizzle in the oil while the processor is running. Store up to 10 days.

To prepare the pasta, cook the orecchiette in boiling, salted water until it's done. Strain and flush with cold water to stop the cooking. Pour the pasta into a large bowl and combine with the remaining ingredients. Add 1 to 2 cups of the dressing, to your taste, toss the salad, and chill it in the refrigerator until serving time.

pair with korbel brut rosé

Simi Winery

16275 healdsburg avenue
healdsburg, ca 95448
707-433-6981

www.simiwinery.com

Many Americans know this dish as spicy clam pasta, although in its native Italy, it's bucatini all'amatriciana con vongole. Translation: thick spaghetti (bucatini), onion/peppers/tomato sauce (all'amatriciana) and clams (vongole). With this recipe, we pay tribute to Tuscans Giuseppe and Pietro Simi, who founded Simi Winery in 1876.

Serves 4

spicy clam pasta
with pancetta, onions & tomato

ingredients

Amatriciana Sauce
1 tablespoon olive oil
2 ¼-inch-thick slices pancetta, chopped
1 small onion, minced
2 cloves garlic, minced
½ teaspoon red pepper flakes
1-½ cups crushed/peeled/seeded tomatoes, with juice
pinch kosher salt and pepper

Pasta
1 pound bucatini
2 tablespoons olive oil

Clams
4 tablespoons unsalted butter
1 pound manila clams, scrubbed and cleaned
½ cup reserved pasta water after cooking
the bucatini
2 tablespoons Italian parsley, chopped
kosher salt and pepper, to taste

directions

To prepare the sauce, in a non-reactive saucepan, sauté the pancetta in the olive oil until the pancetta is golden brown. Transfer the pancetta to paper towels, and keep the oil in the pan. Add the onion and cook until it's lightly golden. Add the garlic and red pepper flakes. Cook for 15 seconds, then add the tomatoes, salt and pepper, and cook over medium-low heat for 20 minutes.

To prepare the pasta, bring a large pot of salted water to a boil. Add the bucatini and cook until the pasta is al dente – firm to the bite. Drain the pasta and run it under cold water. Toss with the olive oil.

To prepare the clams and complete the dish, in a large pot, melt the 4 tablespoons of butter over high heat. Add the clams, reserved pasta water and amatriciana sauce, and cover with the cold pasta, which will act as a lid. When the clams have opened, toss the pasta with the clams. Add the parsley and season with salt and pepper. Serve immediately.

pair with simi pinot noir

Twomey Cellars

3000 westside road
healdsburg, ca 95448
800-505-4850

www.twomeycellars.com

With the bounty of the harvest comes a great variety of heirloom pumpkins. Through October, we like to display our pumpkins for Halloween, but come November, it's time to cook, puree and freeze them for use throughout the holidays and well into winter. For the best flavor, use an heirloom pumpkin or butternut squash for this dish, and not the jack-o-lantern type you carved for Halloween. Prepare and refrigerate the pumpkin puree 1 day ahead.

Serves 4-6

pumpkin gnocchi
with brown butter, walnuts & sage

chef Dominic Orsini

ingredients

1 large heirloom pumpkin
1 large egg
¼ cup grated dry jack cheese
1 teaspoon nutmeg, ground
1-½ cups all-purpose flour, plus some
for dusting
4 tablespoons butter

1 tablespoon fresh sage, chopped
¼ cup walnuts, toasted
1 tablespoon lemon zest
1 tablespoon lemon juice
salt and pepper, to taste
1 chunk aged cow's milk cheese, such as Vella Dry Jack

directions prepare the pumpkin puree 1 day ahead

Cut the pumpkin in half, scoop out the seeds, and place the cut side down on a cookie tray. Bake in a 300° preheated oven for 2 hours, or until the flesh is tender. Scoop out the flesh, puree it in a food processor, and return it to the cookie tray. Bake the puree for an additional 2 hours, stirring every 20 minutes, until it becomes dry, and of the consistency of mashed potatoes. Refrigerate overnight.

To prepare the gnocchi, remove the pumpkin puree from the refrigerator, let it come to room temperature, and place it on a flour-dusted board. Make a well in the middle of the puree with your fingers, and crack the egg into the well. Add the cheese and nutmeg. With your fingers, scramble the egg and slowly incorporate the puree into the egg mixture. Sprinkle ½ of the flour over the mixture and slowly incorporate all the ingredients together.

Fold the mass over on itself and press down again. Sprinkle on more flour, little by little, folding and pressing the dough until it just holds together (try not to knead it.) The dough should give under slight pressure.

Keeping the work surface and dough lightly floured, cut the dough into 4 pieces. Roll each piece into a rope about ½-inch in diameter. Cut the ropes into ½-inch-long pieces. Lightly flour the gnocchi as you cut them.

With a gnocchi board, tilt it at a 45-degree angle. Take each gnocchi piece and squish it lightly with your thumb against the board, while simultaneously pushing it away from you. The dough will roll away and around your thumb, taking on a cupped shape, with ridges on the outer curve from the board and a smooth surface on the inner curve where your thumb was. As you shape the gnocchi, dust them with flour and scatter them on baking sheets lined with parchment paper.

Bring a large pot of salted water to a full boil. Drop in the gnocchi and cook for 2 minutes after they rise to the surface. Strain them and reserve.

Over high heat in a non-stick pan, add the butter, and stir until it turns golden brown. Add the gnocchi and cook until they're lightly browned on one side. Flip them over, add the sage and walnuts to the pan, and cook for an additional 30 seconds. Add the lemon zest, lemon juice, salt and pepper. Stir, and serve with fresh-grated dry jack cheese.

pair with twomey russian river valley pinot noir

entrées

Acorn Winery / Alegría Vineyards

12040 old redwood highway
healdsburg, ca 95448
707-433-6440

www.acornwinery.com

It wouldn't be "A Wine & Food Affair" without an acorn squash-based dish from us. These squash and pork tamales get their spicy kick from four types of chiles – ancho, guajillo, mulato and chipotle. You can find them in most grocery stores that carry Hispanic ingredients, and at Sonoma County farmer's markets.

Serves 6

acorn squash tamales

with red chile-braised pork

ingredients

Pork

8 garlic cloves, unpeeled
4 dried ancho chiles
4 dried guajillo chiles
4 dried mulato chiles
1 chipotle chile
4-½ cups boiling water
1 can (28 ounces) whole peeled tomatoes
1-½ cups warm water
½ teaspoon ground cinnamon
⅛ teaspoon ground cumin

½ teaspoon dried oregano
½ teaspoon dried thyme
coarse salt and pepper, to taste
1 teaspoon cider vinegar
3 tablespoons extra virgin olive oil
1-½ pounds boneless pork shoulder, cut into 2-inch cubes
1 small onion, finely chopped

Tamales

1 cup acorn squash, cut into small dice
1 tablespoon olive oil

1-¾ cups masa harina (corn flour)
1-¼ cups hot water
10 tablespoons chilled vegetable shortening
(such as Crisco)
1-½ teaspoons kosher salt
1 teaspoon baking powder
¼ cup cold vegetable or chicken stock
6 dried corn husks

directions preheat oven to 300°

To prepare the pork, spread the garlic and chiles on a baking sheet and roast until they're softened, about 5 minutes. Let them cool slightly. Tear the chiles into pieces, discarding the stems and seeds. Add the chiles to the boiling water, remove from the heat, and top with a small plate. Let the chiles steam for 30 minutes. Drain them, reserving ½ cup water. Puree the chiles, tomatoes, reserved water and warm water, and set aside.

Peel the garlic. With a mortar and pestle, pound the garlic, spices, herbs, 2 teaspoons of salt and the vinegar into a paste. Heat the oil in a Dutch oven over medium-high heat. Season the pork generously with salt and pepper. Working in batches, cook the pork until it's browned, about 4 minutes per side. Transfer to a plate.

Add the onion to the pot, and cook for 5 minutes. Stir in the paste, and cook for 2 minutes more. Stir in the pork and chile puree, and season with salt and pepper. Bring to a simmer. Cover, place in the oven and cook until the meat is tender, about 3 hours.

To prepare the tamales, toss the acorn squash with the olive oil and roast in a preheated 400° oven for 7-10 minutes, until browned.

Place the corn flour in the bowl of an electric mixer fitted with a paddle attachment. On low speed, add the water in a slow, steady stream until the dough forms a ball. Continue mixing on medium speed for 5 minutes, then transfer the dough to a clean bowl. Cover and refrigerate it for 1 hour.

Return the dough to the mixer and beat for 5 minutes on high speed. While beating, slowly add the cold shortening 2 tablespoons at a time. Continue mixing for 5 more minutes, until the dough is smooth and light. Stop the mixer occasionally to scrape the sides of the bowl with a rubber spatula. Reduce the speed to low and continue to beat.

Meanwhile, combine the salt, baking powder and stock in a small bowl. Slowly add the stock mix to the dough in a steady stream, and continue to mix until it's thoroughly combined. Increase the speed, and mix for 5 minutes longer. Add the roasted acorn squash and mix until just combined.

Press ¼ cup of the dough into a soaked corn husk and fold it over, tucking the ends to hold the filling. Steam for 30 minutes.

To serve, place the tamales on individual plates and cover them with the pork sauce.

pair with acorn heritage vines zinfandel

Bella Vineyards & Wine Caves

9711 west dry creek road
healdsburg, ca 95448
707-473-9171

www.bellawinery.com

We love how the subtle spiciness of this dish
works with our robust Zinfandels –
especially our Lily Hill bottling. It's perfect for
a cool Dry Creek Valley evening.

Serves 4-6

chicken, sausage & shrimp
gumbo with rice

chef Todd Muir, Wine Country Chefs

ingredients

1 cup vegetable oil
1 cup flour
1-½ cups onions, chopped
1 cup celery, chopped
1 cup bell peppers, chopped
1 pound smoked sausage, such as chorizo, cut crosswise into ½-inch slices
1-½ teaspoons salt
1/4 teaspoon cayenne
6 cups chicken stock
½ pound bay shrimp
1 pound boneless chicken meat, cut into 1-inch chunks
salt and pepper
2 cups converted rice
2 tablespoons parsley, chopped
½ cup green onions, chopped

directions

Combine the oil and flour in a large heavy-bottomed pot over medium heat, stirring slowly and constantly for 20 to 25 minutes. This will make a light-brown roux, the color of a coffee latte.

Add the onions, celery and bell peppers to the pot and continue to stir for 4 to 5 minutes, or until the vegetables are wilted. Add the sausage, salt, cayenne and bay shrimp. Continue to cook, stirring, for 3 to 4 minutes. Add the chicken stock. Stir until the roux mixture and stock are well-combined, then bring to a boil. Reduce heat to medium-low and cook, uncovered, for 1 hour, stirring occasionally.

Season the chicken with salt and pepper and add to the pot. Simmer for ½ hour. Add the converted rice, cover, and cook 20 minutes, or until the rice is tender. Remove the pot from the heat and stir in the parsley and green onions. Serve in deep bowls.

pair with bella lily hill estate zinfandel

Bluenose Wines

428 hudson street
healdsburg, ca 95448
707-473-0768

www.bluenosewines.com

This is our favorite Asian-style chicken; its nutty flavors of chocolate and spice pair beautifully with our Zinfandel. Paul Brasset is both chef and winemaker at Bluenose.

Serves 4

spicy zinfandel chicken

chef Paul Brasset

ingredients

2 cups Bluenose Zinfandel
1 cup soy sauce (low sodium)
½ cup tomato sauce
1 tablespoon garlic, chopped
1 tablespoon fresh ginger, grated
1 tablespoon black bean chile sauce
3 tablespoons ground chili paste
3 tablespoons sesame oil
1 tablespoon cayenne pepper
1 teaspoon black pepper
2 pounds chicken legs, thighs and wings
Dijon mustard

directions

In a mixing bowl, prepare a marinade by combining all of the ingredients except the chicken and mustard. Pour the marinade into a large glass baking dish or a large zip lock plastic bag.

Coat the chicken pieces with Dijon mustard and add them to the marinade. Cover the baking dish (or seal the plastic bag), place the chicken in the refrigerator, and allow it to marinate for 2 hours.

Remove the chicken from the marinade and shake off the excess liquid. Preheat a grill and cook the chicken to the desired doneness.

pair with bluenose sonoma county zinfandel

Branham Estate Wines

132 plaza street
healdsburg, ca 95448
707-473-0337

www.branhamwines.com

This dish is an homage to California wine country's Mexican heritage, a desire to fuse cuisines, and a testament to our love of all things pork and cheese. What's not to like? We like this sandwich as an entrée, but you can also slice it into appetizer portions.

Serves 2

rockpile
cheesesteak panini

chef David Ginochio

ingredients

¼ cup olive oil
1 tablespoon red wine vinegar
½ teaspoon dried Mexican oregano
pinch of salt and pepper
4 slices sturdy Italian or sourdough bread, ½-inch thick
6 ounces pork carnitas, either homemade or from your favorite taqueria
6 tablespoons marinated sweet and hot pepper rings, sliced
2 slices provolone or havarti cheese

directions preheat a panini press

Whisk together the oil, vinegar, oregano, salt and pepper, and set aside.

Place 2 slices of bread flat on your work surface and, using a pastry brush, brush the bread on 1 side each with the oil mixture. Place the remaining 2 bread slices on the work surface, and top each with the remaining ingredients, in this order: carnitas, pepper rings and cheese. Arrange the oiled bread on top, oiled side facing up.

Place the sandwiches oil-side-down on the panini press, and brush with the remaining side with oil mixture. Close the press and grill for 4 to 5 minutes, or until the sandwiches are golden brown and the cheese is melted. Then enjoy.

pair with branham estate señal rockpile red

Carol Shelton Wines

3354-b coffey lane
santa rosa, ca 95403
707-575-3441

www.carolshelton.com

Gregory Hallihan, creator of this recipe, says, "Pakistani- and India-influenced flavors work well with Carol Shelton Zinfandels." We agree, and we've tweaked the recipe a bit to complement our Monga Zin. For the best flavor, use Penzey's sweet curry powder and Penzey's tandoori seasoning; they can be purchased at penzeys.com.

Serves 8

karachi beef stew

chef Gregory Hallihan

ingredients

¼ cup canola oil
½ cup all-purpose flour
4 tablespoons mild curry powder
2 tablespoons tandoori seasoning
2 pounds lean stew meat, cut into ¾-inch cubes
1 bottle Carol Shelton Zinfandel, preferably Monga Zin
4 quarts beef stock
1 large or 2 medium yellow onions, chopped
1 stalk celery, chopped
5 large carrots, chopped
8 large red potatoes, chopped into ½-inch pieces
salt and pepper, to taste

directions

Heat the oil in a large stew pot.

Mix the flour with the curry powder in a zip lock plastic bag, add the beef, and tumble the ingredients until the meat is coated. Add the meat to the stew pot and cook until it's browned on all sides. Reserve the flour mixture.

Carefully add the Zinfandel to the pot, then add the beef stock, tandoori seasoning and flour mixture. Bring the pot to a boil, then reduce the heat to simmer, and cook the stew on low for about 2 hours, uncovered.

Add the onions, celery, carrots and potatoes to the pot and simmer for another 30 minutes.

Turn off the heat and let the pot rest 1 hour. Season the stew with salt and pepper to taste, stir through, and serve.

pair with carol shelton monga zin

Chalk Hill Estate Vineyards & Winery

10300 chalk hill road
healdsburg, ca 95448
707-838-4306

www.chalkhill.com

Feuilleté (the word is French, and so is our chef) is a baked puff pastry that can be filled with any number of savory ingredients. Wild-caught Pacific salmon is perfect for feuilletés, and for our Estate Chardonnay.

Serves 4

salmon "feuilleté"

with wild rice & mushrooms

chef Didier Ageorges, Executive Chef

ingredients

1 16-ounce package frozen puff pastry sheets, thawed
½ pound salmon fillet
1 cup wild rice
1 medium yellow onion, minced
½ cup white mushrooms, cleaned and sliced
¼ cup chopped Italian parsley
1 egg yolk
2 tablespoons butter
salt and pepper

directions preheat oven to 325°

Slice the salmon into ¼-inch pieces. In a saucepan over medium heat, melt 1 tablespoon of butter. Add the salmon pieces and sear them 1 minute on each side. Remove the salmon from the heat, and season with salt and pepper.

Cook the rice according to the package directions.

In a sauté pan over low heat, add the remaining butter and sweat the onions until they're translucent. Add the mushrooms and cook until they're soft. Add the parsley.

To assemble the feuilleté, cut 1 pastry sheet into 2 rectangles. On 1 of the rectangles, layer the rice, salmon and mushrooms in the middle, leaving 1 inch on each side. Brush some egg yolk on the edges and cover with the other rectangle. With a knife tip, poke 2 holes in the top for the steam to escape during cooking. Brush egg yolk on the top, and bake for about 40 minutes. Let rest for 20 minutes before serving.

pair with chalk hill estate chardonnay

Davis Family Vineyards

52 front street
healdsburg, ca 95448
707-433-3858

www.daviswines.com

This creation comes to us from John Stewart of Zazu and Bovolo restaurants. Our son, Cooper Davis, worked with the Zazu team to prepare the dish for this year's event. This is a classic French dish, a treasure from Burgundy yet with a Sonoma County twist. If you can't find wild boar, use beef for this recipe.

Serves 6.

wild boar bourguignon

chef John Stewart, Zazu & Bovolo

ingredients

¼ cup olive oil
¼ cup flour
1-½ pounds wild boar shoulder, cut into 1-inch cubes
1-½ pounds pork shoulder, cut into 1-inch cubes
2 medium red onions, chopped
1/2 cup chicken stock
2-½ cups Davis Family Pinot Noir
bay leaf
1 14-ounce can whole tomatoes, roughly chopped
2 carrots, diced
1 cup potatoes, diced
1 tablespoon garlic, chopped
salt and pepper, to taste

directions

In a large sauce pot, add ½ of the oil and heat over medium heat. In small batches, toss the meat cubes in the flour, add them to the pan, and brown the pieces on all sides. Transfer the meat to paper towels.

Discard the oil, wipe the pot clean with a paper towel, and add the remaining oil. Over medium heat, add ½ of the onions and cook them until they're brown. Return the meat to the pot, add the chicken stock, wine and bay leaf, and simmer slowly for about 3 hours, until the meat is tender. Discard the bay leaf.

Add the tomatoes, carrots, potatoes, garlic and remaining red onion to the pot, stir through, and simmer for 30 minutes longer. Season with salt and pepper, and serve the stew with crusty toasted bread.

pair with davis family pinot noir

DeLoach
Vineyards

1791 olivet road
santa rosa, ca 95401
707-526-9111

www.deloachvineyards.com

We like to serve this complexly flavored dish on orzo or penne pasta, but it's also delicious on creamy polenta. The chicken can be marinated as little as two hours, and as long as overnight; the longer the marinating time, the deeper the flavor of the finished dish.

Serves 6-8

braised chicken

with celery, shallots, capers & olives

chef Sue Boy

ingredients

12 chicken thighs, boneless and skinless
2 cups DeLoach Pinot Noir or Zinfandel
8 large celery stalks, trimmed and cut into ½-inch pieces
8 large shallots, peeled and quartered
1 cup kalamata or other brine-cured olives, pitted and halved
½ cup capers, drained
2 tablespoons fresh sage, minced (or 1 tablespoon dry)
2 tablespoons fresh rosemary, removed from stems and minced (or 1 tablespoon dry)
1-½ teaspoons kosher salt
ground black pepper, to taste
2 tablespoons olive oil, or as needed, to brown chicken
1 cup chicken stock
⅓ cup tomato paste

directions

In a large non-reactive pan or dish, combine the chicken, wine, celery, shallots, olives and capers. Sprinkle with the sage, rosemary, salt and pepper, mix well, cover, and refrigerate for 2 to 3 hours, or overnight.

When you're ready to cook, preheat the oven to 350°. Remove the chicken from the marinade, reserving the liquid. Heat the olive oil in a large, heavy skillet and sauté the chicken pieces until they're golden, then set aside.

Deglaze the pan with the chicken stock, scraping the bottom to loosen the browned bits. Add the tomato paste and reserved marinade, and bring to a boil. Remove the pan from the heat.

Arrange the chicken and vegetables in a large, oven-proof casserole with a lid, and add the marinade mixture. Cover and cook for 30 to 40 minutes, stirring occasionally to break up the chicken pieces. Uncover and cook 15 minutes more, or until the chicken is very tender.

To serve, spoon the chicken over orzo or penne pasta, or polenta.

pair with deloach van der kamp vineyard pinot noir

deLorimier Winery

2001 highway 128
geyserville, ca 95441
800-546-7718

www.delorimierwinery.com

Beef bourguignon may have originated in Burgundy (the dish likely was named not for the French region itself, but for the Burgundy wine, Pinot Noir, that was and continues to be a key ingredient). We think Cabernet Sauvignon works just as well, and gives this hearty stew an intense, robust flavor.

Serves 6

beef bourguignon

ingredients

½ cup flour
salt and black pepper
6 ounces smoked bacon, diced
¼ cup peanut oil
3 pounds stew meat, cut in 2-inch cubes
3 cups deLorimier Cabernet Sauvignon
¾ pound crimini mushrooms, quartered
2 medium carrots, diced
6 medium yellow onions, diced
2 bay leaves
¼ cup thyme, chopped
3 garlic cloves, peeled and smashed
6 cups beef stock
water

directions

Season the flour with salt and pepper and set aside.

In a braising pan over medium-high heat, cook the bacon until it's crisp. Transfer the bacon to paper towels to drain, leaving the grease in the pan. Add the peanut oil to the pan and keep the heat on medium-high.

Dust the meat with the seasoned flour and add it to the braising pan, cooking it to get a nice brown color on the exterior. Deglaze the pan with the Cabernet Sauvignon and continue to cook, reducing the liquid by half.

Add the rest of the ingredients to the pan, with enough water to cover by 2 inches. Bring the stew to a boil, cover, and simmer until the meat is tender. Serve it with your favorite starch and vegetable.

pair with delorimier cabernet sauvignon

Dutton Estate Winery

8757 green valley road
sebastopol, ca 95472
707-829-9463

www.duttonestate.com

This hearty fare is a favorite pairing at the winery for our Syrahs. The slow-cooked polenta, which we make in a crock pot, is particularly smooth, and the full-flavored puttanesca sauce is a snap to prepare. The recipe can easily be doubled for a crowd.

Serves 4-6

polenta a la puttanesca

chef Cynthia Newcomb

ingredients

Puttanesca Sauce

¼ cup extra virgin olive oil
4 large garlic cloves, finely chopped
1 28-ounce can chopped and peeled tomatoes in puree
(Muir Glen brand if available)
1/2 cup kalamata olives, halved and pitted
4 anchovy fillets, minced
1-½ tablespoons capers, drained
1 teaspoon dried oregano
½ teaspoon red pepper flakes
2 tablespoons fresh Italian parsley, chopped
parmesan cheese, grated

Polenta

6 cups water
1-½ cups polenta
1-½ teaspoons kosher salt
4 tablespoons butter
4 ounces Vella Dry Jack, Parmigiano-
Reggiano or Pecorino-Romano cheese,
grated (or a mix of these)
pepper

directions

To prepare the polenta, pour the water into a slow cooker and set the control to high. Add the polenta, whisking to separate the grains. Add the salt and cover the cooker with the lid.

Give the polenta a quick stir every 15 minutes or so, until it begins to thicken, which will take 1-½ to 2 hours. Reduce the heat to low and cook for 4 to 5 hours, stirring occasionally. When the polenta is tender and creamy, reset the heat to warm, and hold for up to 10 hours. If at any point the polenta seems too thick, thin it with a little boiling water.

To prepare the puttanesca, heat the oil in a large pot over medium heat. Add the garlic and sauté until it's fragrant, about 3 minutes. Add the tomatoes with puree, olives, anchovies, capers, dried oregano, red pepper flakes and parsley. Simmer the sauce over medium-low heat until it's thickened, about 30 minutes. Season with kosher salt and fresh ground black pepper.

To serve, reset the heat on the crock pot to low and stir the butter and cheese into the polenta. Correct for salt, and season with freshly ground black pepper. Serve the sauce over the polenta.

pair with dutton estate gail ann's syrah

Family Wineries of Dry Creek

4791 dry creek road
healdsburg, ca 95448
707-433-0100

www.familywines.com

Chef Jeff Mall has a love of all things pork, and so do we. There is no better combination of flavors than savory, smoked pork sausage, bacon and white beans to warm you for the cool fall and cold winter – with a glass of one of our wines, of course. You'll need a smoker for this recipe.

Serves 4-6

smoked fennel sausage

with white beans & roasted tomato

chef Jeff Mall, Chef/Owner, Zin Restaurant & Wine Bar

ingredients

6 strips bacon, diced
1 yellow onion, diced
2 cups Great Northern white beans (soaked overnight)
6 Roma tomatoes
1 tablespoon olive oil
1 tablespoon balsamic vinegar
salt and pepper, to taste
6 mild Italian fennel sausages (1-½ pounds)

directions preheat oven to 450°

In a large pot, slowly cook the bacon over medium heat. Add the onions and cook until they're well caramelized. Add the beans and just cover with water. Bring the water to a boil and simmer the beans for 1 to 1½ hours, or until done.

While the beans cook, rinse the tomatoes in cold water, slice them in half and place them in a bowl. Toss the tomatoes with the olive oil, balsamic and salt and pepper. Place them on a baking sheet and roast them in the oven for 20 to 25 minutes, until the tomatoes have started to blacken. Remove them from the oven and let them cool.

When the beans are tender, remove the skins from the tomatoes, cut the flesh into large pieces, and stir them into the beans.

Place the sausages in a smoker for 30 minutes.

To serve, pour the beans onto a platter with edges, or into a bowl. Slice the warm sausages on the diagonal and serve on top of the beans

pair with your favorite red wine from collier falls vineyards, dashe cellars, forth vineyards, lago di merlo vineyards, mietz cellars or philip staley vineyards

Francis Ford Coppola Winery

300 via archimedes
geyserville, ca 95441
707-857-1462

www.franciscoppolawinery.com

Director Martin Scorsese's mother, Catherine, had minor roles in several of his films, but Francis Ford Coppola remembers her best as a great cook. In fact, she published a cookbook, "Italianamerican: The Scorsese Family Cookbook," in 1996. This is one of Francis' favorite recipes from Catherine Scorsese.

Serves 4-6

mrs. scorsese's
lemon chicken

chef **Francis Ford Coppola**

ingredients

1 tablespoon olive oil
1 3-pound chicken, cut into serving pieces (leg and thigh separated and breast into 3 pieces)
3 large garlic cloves
1-½ cups lemon juice
salt and pepper, to taste
1/4 cup water
2 tablespoons fresh oregano, torn, plus 3 additional sprigs

directions preheat oven to 400°

Coat the bottom of a cast iron baking dish with the olive oil. Peel and cut the garlic cloves into thirds. Evenly distribute the garlic pieces in the pan.

Rinse the chicken and pat the pieces dry with paper towels. Arrange the chicken in the baking dish, skin-side-up.

In a small bowl, combine the lemon juice, salt and pepper. Taste the mixture, and if it's too sour or acidic, add water to your taste. Pour the lemon juice mixture over the chicken, turning to coat all sides. Add the torn oregano and sprigs to the top (skin side) of the chicken.

Put the baking pan into the oven and cook the chicken until the skin is browned, basting occasionally with the pan juices, for approximately 40 to 45 minutes.

Transfer the chicken to a serving dish and pour the pan drippings into a sauceboat, to be served separately.

pair with francis ford coppola director's cut russian river valley chardonnay or sonoma coast pinot noir

Hanna Winery

9280 highway 128
healdsburg, ca 95448
707-431-4310

5353 occidental road
santa rosa, ca 95401
707-575-3371

www.hannawinery.com

We honeymooned in Barcelona, so I'm naturally a fan of all things Spanish. This recipe is similar to paella with its rice base, but depends on briny shrimp and spicy chorizo for its savory flavor. Equally delicious with white and red wine, this dish is a real crowd pleaser.

Serves 4-6

spanish shrimp & chorizo

ingredients

1 tablespoon olive oil
12 ounces Spanish chorizo, thinly sliced
1 large onion, chopped
1 large red bell pepper, finely chopped
3 cloves garlic, finely chopped
1 celery stalk, finely chopped
1-½ cups short-grain rice
3 cups fish or chicken broth (if unsalted, add more salt to the dish)
1 14-ounce can tomatoes, or 3 fresh tomatoes, chopped
½ teaspoon cayenne
pinch saffron threads
1 teaspoon salt
1 cup green peas
1-½ pounds raw shrimp, peeled and deveined

directions

In a large Dutch oven or casserole, heat the olive oil over medium heat until it shimmers. Add the chorizo slices and sauté until they're caramelized, about 5 minutes. Remove the chorizo to a dish.

Add the onion to the pan and sauté until it's translucent, about 3 minutes. Add the red pepper, garlic and celery and sauté 3 minutes more, until the vegetables soften somewhat and become fragrant. Add the rice and sauté for several minutes more.

Add the broth, tomatoes, reserved chorizo, cayenne, saffron and salt, reduce the heat to low, and cover. Cook 20 minutes, until the rice is just cooked through. Taste and adjust the seasoning if necessary

Add the peas and shrimp, toss gently to combine with the rice mixture, cover and let steam for 2 to 3 minutes, until the shrimp are just cooked through. Serve immediately.

pair with hanna russian river valley sauvignon blanc, alexander valley cabernet sauvignon or bismark mountain vineyard zinfandel

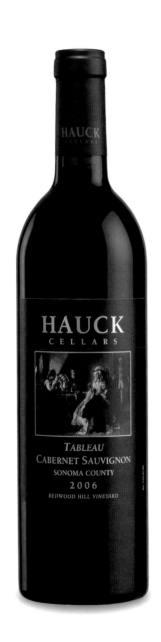

Hauck Cellars

223 center street
healdsburg, ca 95448
707-473-9065

www.hauckcellars.com

This version of beef stew with mushrooms is our go-to dinner party recipe. It can be made a day in advance, is fool-proof, and is a winter-time staple at our house. I used to be able to use this recipe as a bargaining tool with Greg, but now he knows how to make it, too. Open two bottles of wine: one for you and one for the stew!

Serves 6

hauck cellars'
cabernet boeuf forestier

chef Jennifer Hauck

ingredients

2 pounds boneless beef, cut into cubes
3 tablespoons flour
2 tablespoons butter
2 tablespoons vegetable oil
4 ounces bacon, sliced into ¼-inch strips
2 cups pearl onions (frozen is fine)
2 cups mushrooms, quartered
2 cups baby carrots
3 garlic cloves, minced
14 ounces beef stock
1 bottle Hauck Cabernet Sauvignon or other dry red wine
2 bay leaves
salt and pepper
sugar

directions

Place the beef cubes in a zip lock bag with 2 tablespoons of flour and shake until the meat is coated on all sides.

In a large stock pot, melt the butter and vegetable oil together over medium-high heat, add the meat, and brown it on all sides, working in batches. Season with salt and pepper during this process. Set the beef aside in a bowl.

In the same pot, brown the bacon. Add the onions, mushrooms, carrots and garlic, and sauté over medium/low heat until the vegetables begin to brown, about 15 minutes.

Sprinkle the mixture with the remaining 1 tablespoon of flour, stir, and cook about 3 minutes more, stirring. Add the beef broth, ½ cup at a time, stirring after each addition. Then add the wine, slowly stirring after each cup or so. Bring the stew to a boil, add the bay leaves and beef (with the accumulated juices), cover, and simmer for 1 hour. The beef should be covered with liquid. If not, add more wine or broth.

Uncover the pot and simmer until the beef is tender and the sauce thickened, about 30 minutes. Taste for seasoning; I always add a teaspoon of salt or more and sometimes a teaspoon to a tablespoon of sugar, depending on the winey-ness of the stew. Salt brings out the flavor in the ingredients, so be sure to taste the sauce before serving.

pair with hauck cellars alexander valley cabernet sauvignon or tableau sonoma county cabernet sauvignon

Hawley Wines

36 north street
healdsburg, ca 95448
707-473-9500

www.hawleywine.com

Begin preparing this classic French meat-and-beans casserole a day in advance. Overnight, soak the white beans and cure the pork shoulder and shanks. Duck confit legs can be purchased at most butcher shops; order them in advance.

Serves 12

patrick's cassoulet

chef Patrick Martin, Chef/Owner, Restaurant Charcuterie

ingredients

3 pounds dried white beans, soaked overnight
3 pounds trimmed pork shoulder, cut in 2-inch cubes
2 fresh pork shanks
kosher salt for curing the pork
1-½ cups olive oil
4 red onions, peeled and diced
3 carrots, peeled and diced
½ cup garlic, chopped
½ cup herbs de provence
3 dried bay leaves
½ cup tomato paste
black pepper, to taste
12 cooked duck confit legs
2 pounds pork sausages, blanched and sliced
2 cups bread crumbs

directions begin the recipe 1 day in advance

Soak the beans overnight. Liberally salt the pork shoulder and shanks with kosher salt and allow them to cure overnight in the refrigerator.

The next day, rinse and dry the pork. In a large pot, heat the olive oil and sauté the cured pork until the pieces are browned on the outside, and set aside. Preheat the oven to 375°. In the same pot, add the onions, carrots, garlic and herbs, and sauté for 3 minutes. Add the tomato paste. Rinse the beans, put them back in their pot, and add the sautéed pork. Cover with water and bring to a boil. Then reduce to a simmer, and cook for 3 hours, or until the beans are tender. Season with pepper.

Place the duck confit legs and sliced sausages in a baking dish, and top them with the bean mixture and bread crumbs. Bake for 30 minutes, or until golden, and serve.

pair with hawley pinot noir

Hobo Wine Company

132 plaza street
healdsburg, ca 95448
707-473-0337

www.hobowines.com

The folks who own Kogi BBQ, a Los Angeles taco truck, created the Korean taco and made it famous. We had our first Korean taco at the Outside Lands music festival in San Francisco. We created our own version to pair with our Pinot Noir. The Korean barbecue sauce is adapted from steamykitchen.com.

Serves 24

korean bbq

pulled pork tacos

with pickled cucumber

chef Lynn Wheeler

ingredients

Dry Rub
¼ cup packed brown sugar
½ cup sweet or hot paprika
¼ cup chili powder
¼ cup salt
¼ cup cracked black pepper
2 tablespoons ground red pepper

Pork
1 bone-in pork shoulder (about 4 pounds)
2 tablespoons vegetable oil

Pickled Cucumber
1 large English cucumber, very thinly sliced
2 tablespoons rice vinegar
1 teaspoon sugar
½ teaspoon fresh chile pepper, finely minced (or dried flakes)
pinch salt

BBQ Sauce
2 tablespoons Korean fermented hot pepper paste (gochujang)
3 tablespoons sugar
2 tablespoons soy sauce
2 teaspoons rice wine vinegar
2 teaspoons sesame oil (untoasted)
1-2 teaspoons Sriracha hot sacue, depending on taste

Assembly
2 teaspoons sesame seeds
24 4-inch corn tortillas

directions

To prepare the dry rub, combine all the ingredients in a small bowl. Rub the pork with the dry rub, wrap the meat in foil, and refrigerate for up to 24 hours.

To prepare the cucumbers, place the slices in a bowl. Add the remaining ingredients, mix well, and chill in the refrigerator for 1 hour or up to 3 days.

To prepare the sauce, combine all the ingredients in a small bowl, mix well, and refrigerate until ready to use.

To cook the meat, position the rack in the center of the oven, and preheat the oven to 325°. Heat the vegetable oil in a Dutch oven or large oven-proof pot over medium heat. Brown the meat on all sides. Cover the pot, put it in the oven, and bake until the meat can be shredded with a fork, about 3 to 3-½ hours.

When the meat is done, skim the fat from the pan juices. Shred the meat and mix with the pan juices and the Korean BBQ sauce.

To serve, put 2 tablespoons of meat on a tortilla, then 1 tablespoon of pickled cucumber and a sprinkle of sesame seeds.

pair with folk machine central coast pinot noir

Hop Kiln Winery

6050 westside road
healdsburg, ca 95448
707-433-6491

www.hopkilnwinery.com

Don't worry if you cannot pronounce the name of this recipe; just know that it's rice with shrimp and sausage, and that it's delicious. At "A Wine & Food Affair", Chef Renzo will serve this dish, using his authentic Italian pronunciation. Buon appetito!

Serves 4-6

riso con gamberi e salsicce

chef Renzo Veronese

ingredients

½ teaspoon saffron
¼ cup hot water
20 large shrimp, peeled and deveined
kosher salt and freshly ground pepper
½ cup vegetable oil
8 ounces Italian sausage, without casing
1 tablespoon smoked paprika
3 cloves garlic, minced
3 dried bay leaves
1 small onion, minced
3 medium tomatoes, minced
1 cup HKG Chardonnay
6 cups chicken broth
2-½ cups short-grain rice
1 cup fresh or frozen peas
3 roasted red peppers, cut into ½-inch strips

directions

In a small bowl, place the saffron and hot water, and let stand for 15 minutes.

Season the shrimp with salt and pepper. Heat ¼ cup of the oil in a large sauté pan over medium-high heat. Add the sausage and cook until it's nearly done, about 5 minutes. Drain most of the fat from the pan. In a separate pan, heat the remaining ¼ cup of oil over medium-high heat and sauté the shrimp briefly, then set aside.

In the sausage pan, add the paprika, garlic, bay leaves and onion and cook, stirring often, until the onions soften. Add the tomatoes and cook for 5 minutes. Add the reserved saffron "tea," the wine and broth, season with salt, and bring to a boil over high heat.

Sprinkle in the rice, distribute it evenly with a spoon, and add the peas and roasted peppers. Cook, without stirring, until the rice has absorbed most of the liquid, 10 to 12 minutes. Reduce the heat to low, add the shrimp, and cook, without stirring, until the liquid is absorbed and the rice is al dente. Remove the pan from the heat, cover it with foil and let it sit for 5 minutes before serving.

pair with hkg russian river valley estate chardonnay

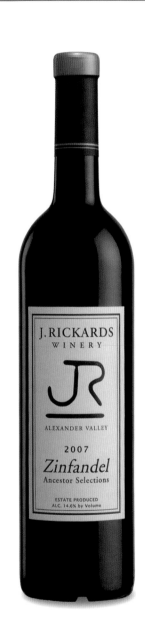

J. Rickards Winery

24505 chianti road
cloverdale, ca 95425
707-758-3441

www.jrwinery.com

This dish is a big hit with our friends on our annual bottling day. Ever since Jim and I started making wine in 1991, we've asked folks to help bottle a barrel or two. Many are musicians and we always have a wide variety of music playing to keep the tempo upbeat. The number has risen from a dozen to almost 40 friends, so making a big "hot dish" is a given. I've pared this version down to feed a smaller group.

Serves 6

jazzy jambalaya

chef Eliza Rickards

ingredients

Seasoning Mix
2 bay leaves
1 teaspoon cayenne
1-½ teaspoons salt
1-½ teaspoons white pepper
1 teaspoon dried thyme
½ teaspoon black pepper
½ teaspoon dried sage

Jambalaya Base
1 tablespoon butter
1 pound andouille sausage, cut into bite-size pieces
1 pound boneless chicken thighs,
cut into bite-size pieces
1 pound shrimp, peeled and deveined (size 26-30),
tails removed
1 cup onion, diced
1 cup celery, diced
1 cup green bell pepper, diced
1 tablespoon garlic, chopped
12-ounce can diced tomatoes in sauce
2-½ cups chicken stock
1-½ cups long-grain rice

directions preheat oven to 350°

To prepare the seasoning mix, combine all the ingredients in a bowl and set aside.

To prepare the jambalaya base, melt the butter in a large saucepan over medium-high heat. Add the sausage and cook about 3 minutes, until the meat starts to brown. Add the chicken and cook until the pieces turn brown, about 5 minutes. Add the shrimp and cook until they're pink, about 4 minutes, stirring frequently.

Stir in the seasoning mix and ½ each of the onion, celery, bell peppers and garlic. Cook until the vegetables are tender, about 6 minutes. Stir in the tomatoes and their sauce, and cook 1 more minute. Mix in the remaining vegetables and remove from the heat. Add the chicken stock and rice, and mix well.

Transfer the mixture to an ungreased baking pan and bake, uncovered, for about 1 hour, or until all the liquid has evaporated. Stir periodically and allow the jambalaya to sit for 5 to 10 minutes before serving.

pair with j. rickards ancestor selections zinfandel

Kachina Vineyards

4551 dry creek road
healdsburg, ca 95448
707-332-7917

www.kachinavineyards.com

This is a melt-in-your-mouth dish from the South. The coffee adds complexity and earthy flavors that complement big, bold red wines such as Cabernet Sauvignon and Zinfandel. This is a great food and wine pairing to share with friends and family sitting around a cozy fire on a cool, fall evening.

Serves 8

braised pork shoulder

with red eye gravy

chef Mike Matson, Vintage Valley Catering

ingredients

3 pounds boneless pork shoulder
1 tablespoon cumin
salt and pepper, to taste
1 pound Applewood smoked bacon
3 medium onions, diced
½ bottle Kachina Cabernet Sauvignon
1 cup brewed coffee
3 cups tomatoes, diced
2 tablespoons chili paste
1 tablespoon dried sage
1 gallon water
salt and pepper, to taste

directions

Cut the pork into 2-inch cubes. Season it with the cumin, salt and pepper.

Dice the bacon and crisp it in a large sauté pan over medium heat. Remove the bacon and set it aside, leaving the bacon grease in the pan.

Brown the pork in the bacon grease. Remove the meat and reserve with the bacon.

Sauté the onions in the same pan. Return the pork to the pan, deglaze with the wine and coffee, and reduce the liquid by ½. Add the tomatoes, chili paste, sage and water. Bring the mixture to a boil and simmer until the meat is almost tender.

Remove the pork from the broth and set aside. Puree the broth, which becomes the red eye gravy, and add the pork back to it. Serve the meat and gravy over cheesy polenta or grits.

pair with kachina cabernet sauvignon

Locals Tasting Room

21023-a geyserville avenue
geyserville, ca 95441
707-857-4900

www.tastelocalwines.com

We are fortunate to have as a neighbor chef Dino Bugica and his wonderful Diavola Pizzeria-Salumeria. He was generous enough to give us this recipe for what he calls, in his native Italian, brasato di manzo al vino rosso. We call it darn good.

Serves 6

cocoa-crusted beef

braised in red wine

chef Dino Bugica, Diavola Pizzeria-Salumeria

ingredients

2 pounds chuck roast
salt and pepper
¼ cup flour
¼ cup unsweetened cocoa powder
3 tablespoons olive oil
3 tablespoons unsalted butter
1 yellow onion, chopped
1 carrot, peeled and chopped
1 celery stalk, chopped
2 tablespoons parsley, chopped
2 tablespoons fresh rosemary, chopped
2 bay leaves
2 cloves garlic, chopped
1 bottle dry red wine
½ cup pine nuts
½ cup currants

directions

Season the chuck roast with salt and pepper. On a large plate, stir together the flour and cocoa. Dust the roast on all sides with the flour-cocoa mixture, shaking off the excess and reserving it.

In a heavy skillet, heat the olive oil over high heat and add the roast, browning it on all sides, approximately 10 to 15 minutes. Set aside.

In a Dutch oven, melt the butter over medium-high heat. Add the onion, carrot, celery, parsley, rosemary, bay leaves and garlic. Sauté until the vegetables are softened, 8 to 10 minutes. Add the browned meat and the wine, and bring to a gentle boil. Reduce the heat to low, cover and simmer until the meat is tender, approximately 2-½ hours.

Transfer the meat to a carving board and cover. If the remaining sauce is too thin, reduce it over high heat to a satisfactory consistency, adding 2 tablespoons of the reserved flour-cocoa mixture as the sauce reduces. Add the pine nuts and currants.

Serve with polenta and braised cabbage.

pair with your favorite red wine from locals

Longboard Vineyards

5 fitch street
healdsburg, ca 95448
707-433-3473

www.longboardvineyards.com

Cassoulet and Syrah are perfect for a cold winter night after a surf session. Even if you don't surf, you'll love this pairing.

Serves 6-8

bistro m cassoulet

chef **Matthew Bousquet, Chef/Owner, Bistro M**

ingredients

3 tablespoons olive oil
1 tablespoon garlic, chopped
½ pound mirepoix (onions, celery, carrots, diced)
2 pounds sausage de Toulouse, cut into bite-sized pieces
1 pound lamb shank, cooked
4 tablespoons fresh thyme, chopped
1 pound white beans, cooked
salt, to taste
1 pound duck confit
2 tablespoons butter, softened
2 cups bread crumbs

directions preheat oven to 375°

Heat a large pot over medium-high heat and add the oil and garlic. Cook the garlic until it becomes fragrant, add the mirepoix, and sweat the vegetables until they're just tender. Add the sausage and lamb shank. Add the thyme and beans, and season with salt.

In a mixing bowl, combine the bread crumbs with the butter and blend until you get a coarse meal consistency. Sprinkle the crumbs liberally over the cassoulet and bake, uncovered, for 45 minutes. Top with the duck confit and bake for another 15 minutes, and serve.

pair with longboard dakine syrah

Merriam
Vineyards

11654 los amigos road
healdsburg, ca 95448
707-433-4032

www.merriamvineyards.com

Boneless lamb shoulder (preferably from
Sonoma County, of course) becomes
melt-in-your-mouth tender when it's braised
in a wine-based liquid for 3 hours.

Serves 6

tuscan braised
lamb shoulder
with brown butter-sage polenta

chef Liza Hinman, Chef, Santi Restaurant

ingredients

Braised Lamb
5 pounds boneless lamb shoulder, tied
salt and pepper
3 tablespoons olive oil
2 cloves garlic, finely chopped
¼ cup celery, diced
¼ cup carrot, diced
¼ cup yellow onion, diced
1 tablespoon fresh rosemary, chopped
1 tablespoon fresh sage, chopped
1 pinch nutmeg, freshly ground
1 pinch clove, freshly ground
1 bottle high-quality red wine (preferably Merriam)
4 cups chicken stock
1 cup San Marzano tomatoes, crushed by hand

Brown Butter Polenta
4 cups whole milk
4 cups water
1 bunch sage, bundled
1-½ cups medium ground polenta
¼ cup sweet butter, cubed

directions preheat oven to 325°

To prepare the lamb, season the tied shoulder all over with salt and pepper. Heat the oil in a large Dutch oven over high heat. Add the lamb and cook, turning occasionally, until the meat is browned all over, 8 to 10 minutes. Remove the lamb and set it aside.

Pour out any excess oil from the pot and discard. Add the remaining tablespoon of oil and heat it over medium-high heat. Stir in the garlic, celery, carrot, onion, herbs, nutmeg and clove. Season with salt and pepper, and cook for 1 minute. Return the lamb to the pot and add the wine, chicken stock and tomatoes. Bring the mixture to a boil, cover, and transfer to the oven. Cook until the lamb is fork-tender, 2-½ to 3 hours. Transfer the lamb to a platter and keep it warm until you're ready to serve the dish.

To prepare the sauce, warm the Dutch oven on the stove over low heat and reduce the liquid, stirring, until it thickens, about 3 minutes. Keep it warm.

To prepare the polenta, add the water, milk and sage bundle to a large pot. Bring it just to a boil, and slowly pour the polenta into the milk, while stirring. Turn the heat to low, and continue to stir until the polenta is totally incorporated into the milk, about 5 minutes. Allow the polenta to simmer, on low, for 25 minutes, stirring frequently. Season with salt, to taste.

Place the butter in a pan and melt it over low heat. When the butter reaches a light brown color, remove it from the heat and stir it into the polenta. Add the cheese and remove the sage bundle. Keep the polenta warm until you're ready to serve the dish.

To serve, remove the twine from the lamb and slice the meat. Place the slices on a bed of the polenta and add the sauce.

pair with merriam vineyards cabernet franc

Mueller Winery

6301 starr road
windsor, ca 95492
707-837-7399

www.muellerwine.com

Traditionally, we celebrate fall with this savory meal. During harvest, there is very little time for food preparation. However, harvest meals are one of the attractions that keep the Mueller crush crew coming back. Season after season, members of our family return to help with all of the "glamorous" crush duties. Endless, sticky hours of punching down, pumping over and cleaning, cleaning, cleaning, are rewarded with special meals, great wine and the "snack cabinet."

Serves 6

chef shari's

beef bourguignon

chef Shari Sarabi

ingredients

2-½ pounds boneless beef (rump or chuck)
flour, for dusting the beef
3 tablespoons olive oil
1 clove garlic
1-¾ cups Mueller Emily's Cuvée Pinot Noir
water
1-½ teaspoons salt
1 bay leaf
3 sprigs parsley
3 strips bacon, diced
½ cup onion, coarsely chopped
1 tablespoon tomato paste
¼ teaspoon ground pepper
20 medium-sized mushroom caps
2 tablespoon butter

directions preheat oven to 325°

Cut the beef into large cubes and roll them in the flour.

In a large skillet, heat the olive oil over high heat. Add the beef to the skillet and brown the cubes on all sides. Add the garlic and cook for 1 minute. Transfer the beef mixture to a 2-quart casserole or Dutch oven.

Add the Pinot Noir, salt, bay leaf and parsley, and just enough water to cover the meat. Cover the casserole and cook in the oven for 2 hours.

In a frying pan, cook the bacon lightly, add the onions, and fry until the onions are light brown and the bacon is crisp. Add the bacon mixture to the cooked beef, along with the tomato paste and pepper. Stir until blended, and cook for another ½ hour, or until the meat is tender. In a clean sauté pan, melt the butter over medium heat and add the mushroom caps. Cook the mushrooms until they're tender and arrange over the top of the casserole. Serve the dish hot, with a loaf of fresh, crusty bread.

pair with mueller emily's cuvee russian river valley pinot noir

Route 128 Vineyards & Winery

21079 geyserville avenue, suite 2
geyserville, ca 95441
707-696-0004

www.route128winery.com

Dried hibiscus flowers give these ribs an exotic aroma and flavor. The dish is delicious, yet not quite complete, without them. In the summer, try substituting fresh blackberries for the honey.

Serves 4-6

hibiscus-honey-braised

short ribs

with white bean puree

chef Rian Rinn

ingredients

Short Ribs
3 pounds beef short ribs,
cut in 2-inch segments across the bone
salt, for seasoning
3 tablespoons peanut or canola oil
¼ cup honey
⅛ teaspoon cayenne
2 carrots, peeled and cut in 1-inch lengths
5 cloves garlic, crushed with skin on
1 medium onion, cut in eighths
30 coriander seeds
¼ teaspoon anise seed
1 bay leaf
15 black peppercorns
2 allspice berries
5 whole cloves
¾ bottle Route 128 Syrah
½ cup dried hibiscus flowers
1 quart chicken stock

Beans
3 cups dried cannellini beans
1 onion, quartered
1 carrot, quartered
sprig of thyme
2 garlic cloves
1 bay leaf
2 whole cloves
1 lemon, halved

directions preheat oven to 375°

Season the meat generously with salt (but not pepper). In a large sauté pan over high heat, heat the oil. Sear the ribs on all sides, until they're golden brown. Remove them from the pan and drain the fat, but do not rinse the pan.

On medium-low heat, deglaze the pan with the honey and cayenne. When the honey begins to foam, add the carrots, garlic, onion, coriander, anise and bay leaf. Combine the ingredients and cook until the onions are opaque. Grind together the peppercorns, allspice and cloves, and add them to the pan. Add the Syrah.

Settle the ribs back into the liquid and continue cooking until the mixture is reduced by half. Add the hibiscus flowers and cover the meat with chicken stock. Cook 2 hours, uncovered, in the oven.

To prepare the beans, in a large pot, cover all the ingredients with water, 3 level fingers above the surface of the beans. Cook on low for 1-1/2 to 3 hours, adding liquid, if necessary. When done, the beans should be tender but not mushy.

Drain the beans, reserving the liquid. Discard the vegetables and herbs. In a food processor or with an immersion blender, puree the beans. Slowly add some of the reserved liquid until the desired consistency is achieved. The bean puree will be smooth and form soft peaks. Serve with the short ribs.

pair with route 128 syrah

Sbragia Family Vineyards

9990 dry creek road
geyserville, ca 95441
707-473-2992

www.sbragia.com

This sauce – "sugo" in Italian – makes a large amount. There will be plenty left over to serve with pasta or to use for another meal.

Serves 10

manna meatballs in sugo

chef **Marisa Manna**

ingredients

Meatballs
5 tablespoons butter
2 tablespoons olive oil
1 small yellow onion, finely chopped
2 garlic cloves, minced
1 pound ground beef
½ pound ground veal
½ pound ground pork
¾ cup Parmigiano-Reggiano cheese, grated
¼ cup Italian parsley, finely chopped
1 cup plain bread crumbs
1 cup Italian bread crumbs
2 eggs, lightly beaten
½ teaspoon red pepper flakes
½ cup ricotta cheese
1-½ tablespoons fennel seeds
2 teaspoons ground mustard
3 tablespoons whole milk
sea salt and fresh ground pepper, to taste

Sugo (sauce)
1 small yellow onion, chopped
3 garlic gloves, crushed and chopped
1 bay leaf
½ cup dry red wine
2 28-ounce cans Roma tomatoes, crushed
6 basil leaves, julienne cut
sea salt and fresh ground pepper, to taste

directions

To prepare the meatballs, in a large frying pan over medium-high heat, add 3 tablespoons of the butter and 1 tablespoon of the oil. Add the onion and garlic and sauté until they're softened and golden, about 5 minutes. Pour the mixture into a large mixing bowl and let cool for 5 minutes.

Add the ground meat, eggs, red pepper flakes, ricotta cheese, fennel seeds, mustard, milk, Parmigiano-Reggiano, salt and pepper to the bowl. Using your (clean) hands, mix all the ingredients together until they're well blended. Shape the meat mixture into 2-inch balls, placing them on a large tray.

In the same frying pan over medium-high heat, add the remaining 2 tablespoons of butter and 1 tablespoon of oil. Add the meatballs and cook, turning them over occasionally, until they're crisp on all sides, about 15 to 20 minutes. Transfer the meatballs to a large tray. Keep the fat in the frying pan.

To prepare the sauce, return the pan with the remaining fat to medium heat, add the onion and garlic, and sauté until they're soft and golden. Add the bay leaf. Pour in the wine to deglaze the pan, letting the wine reduce, about 3 to 5 minutes. Add the tomatoes and their juices, and stir well. Cook until the sauce thickens, about 15 minutes, then stir in the basil.

To serve, add the meatballs to the sauce and serve warm. Garnish with Parmigiano-Reggiano.

pair with sbragia family vineyards italo's vineyard zinfandel

Sheldon Wines

1301 cleveland avenue
santa rosa, ca 95401
707-477-6879

www.sheldonwines.com

There's nothing quite like coming home, cold, wet and tired from a long autumn day at the winery, to the scent of slow-braised short ribs. One of our favorite fall recipes, as the rains return and nights get longer, this red-wine-friendly dish is a great way to warm the soul.

Serves 4

petite sirah-braised
short ribs & gremolata

chef Dylan Sheldon

ingredients

Gremolata
¼ cup parsley, finely chopped
zest of ½ lemon, finely chopped
1 garlic clove, finely chopped

Short Ribs
4-5 pounds beef short ribs
salt and pepper
2 large yellow onions, roughly chopped
2 leeks, washed, tops discarded, roughly chopped
1 tablespoon olive oil
1 carrot, chopped
2 Roma tomatoes, chopped
6 cloves garlic, crushed
3 bay leaves
6 sprigs thyme
½ bunch parsley
2 cups Petite Sirah
2-3 cups beef broth

directions preheat oven to 425°

To prepare the gremolata, mix all the ingredients in a small bowl and refrigerate until the ribs are in their final cooking stage.

To prepare the ribs, cut them into squares, so that each piece has a bone. Trim the fat and season generously with salt and pepper. Roast the ribs bone-side-down for 20 minutes.

Meanwhile, in a sauté pan, cook the onions, leeks and carrot in the olive oil until they are slightly softened. Add the tomatoes, garlic and herbs, and sauté a few minutes more.

Spread the vegetables in a baking dish big enough to hold the roasted ribs. Put the ribs bone-side-up on top of the vegetables. Add the wine and just enough stock to barely cover the ribs. Cover the dish tightly with foil and put it back in the hot oven.

After 20 minutes, reduce the heat to 350° and loosen the foil. Start checking for doneness after 1 to 1-½ hours; the ribs should be tender and nearly falling from the bone. Uncover them and turn them bone-side-down. Pour off and strain the braising juices and save in a bowl. Raise the heat to 425° again and return the ribs for final browning, approximately 10 minutes more.

To serve, remove the ribs from the oven and pour the braising juices over the meat. Scatter the gremolata over the ribs and serve immediately.

pair with sheldon petite sirah

Suncé Winery

1839 olivet road
santa rosa, ca 95401
707-526-9463

www.suncewinery.com

Sweating the onions produces a more
rounded, sweet flavor that brings out
the sweetness of the lamb. Letting the
ground mixture rest overnight infuses flavor
throughout the meat and acts as a marinade.
"Fire and Ice" – the combination
of hot cayenne and cooling mint in the
yogurt dipping sauce – lends a dramatic
note to the entire dish.

Serves 10 to 15

lamb lollipops

chef Zoran Matulic, Chef/Owner, Hamilton Cafe

ingredients

Lamb Skewers

3 tablespoons olive oil
2 yellow onions, diced
5 pounds ground lamb
3 garlic cloves, minced
½ cup mint leaves, minced
2 tablespoons Spanish paprika
1-½ tablespoons Dijon mustard
2 teaspoons salt, or to taste
1-½ teaspoons pepper, or to taste
6-inch bamboo skewers

Spicy Yogurt Dressing

4 cups plain Greek yogurt
1 teaspoon cayenne
2 tablespoons mint leaves, finely chopped
salt and pepper, to taste

directions begin this recipe 1 day in advance

To prepare the lamb, in a sauté pan, heat the olive oil over low heat. Add the onions and cook them slowly, until they're translucent. Drain any excess oil.

Break up the lamb into a large bowl. Add the cooked onions, garlic, mint, paprika, mustard, salt and pepper, kneading them into the meat. Cover the bowl and refrigerate the lamb overnight.

When you're ready to serve the dish, soak the skewers in water, so that they don't burn on the grill. Divide the lamb mixture into equal pieces. Shape each piece into 1-inch diameter log, approximately 3 inches long. Thread each log lengthwise onto a skewer.

Place the skewers on a hot grill and cook for about 5 minutes, turning once, until the lamb is medium-rare.

To prepare the yogurt dressing, mix together all the ingredients in a bowl and serve at room temperature with the lamb skewers and ajvar, a roasted-pepper relish that can be purchased at ethnic gourmet stores.

pair with suncé zora's vineyard pinot noir

Terroirs Artisan Wines

21001 geyserville avenue
geyserville, ca 95441
707-857-4101

www.terroirsartisanwines.com

Terroir is the sense of place that defines wine, food and experiences. During the holidays, our family always makes a dish our great, great grandparents brought with them from Cornwall, England, to California: cornish pasties. They are rich meat pies stuffed with root vegetables and beef, traditionally served with a sweet pickle. Our pasties reflect the way we make wine – Old World meets New. All the ingredients for this dish can be found within 50 miles of our vineyards. We are strong advocates of the locavore movement and think you will agree that the freshest ingredients make the finest food.

Serves 4

cornish pasties

chef Bruce Riezenman, Park Avenue Catering

ingredients

Crust
4 cups unbleached flour
pinch of salt
2-½ sticks cold, unsalted butter, cut into tiny cubes
½ cup cold water

Filling
1 large Yukon Gold potato, thinly sliced
1 large rutabaga, thinly sliced
¾ pound beef flank steak, diced
1-½ small white onions, finely chopped
kosher salt and pepper
2 teaspoons butter
1 tablespoon flour
1 tablespoon milk
1 egg, beaten with 1 tablespoon cold water

directions preheat oven to 425°

To prepare the crust, combine the flour and salt in a large bowl. Add the butter and work it with your fingertips until the texture looks like coarse meal. Sprinkle with water and quickly assemble the dough into a ball. Wrap it in cloth and refrigerate.

To prepare the pasties, dust the work surface with flour. Roll out the dough in a 12-inch by 12-inch square. Cut the square in 4 equal pieces in a cross shape. Lift each piece with a spatula so it does not stick to the surface. Each piece will fold in half on the diagonal.

On each half, place a layer of potato, rutabaga, meat and onions, leaving a ¼-inch clean border around the edges. Place ½ teaspoon of butter in the center of each pasty, dust each with flour, and sprinkle with salt and pepper. Brush all the edges with milk. Fold the empty half of the pastry over the filling and squeeze the edges firmly together to seal. Twist the edges slightly, using your index and thumb to create a rolling hill pattern. Brush each pasty with the beaten egg wash.

With a sharp knife, cut a ½-inch slit in the center of each pasty. Bake for 20 minutes, reduce the oven temperature to 325°, and bake for 40 minutes more.

Serve the pasties with a side of pickle from our local grower, Soda Rock Farm.

pair with palmeri van ness vineyard syrah

Topel Wines

125 matheson street
healdsburg, ca 95448
707-433-4166

www.topelwines.com

This recipe is best prepared a day or two
before serving. If desired, scatter a mixture of
chopped parsley, finely chopped preserved
lemon zest and finely chopped garlic over
the ribs right before serving. These ribs
are wonderful served with either buttermilk
mashed potatoes or creamy polenta, and
sautéed greens, such as spinach,
red kale or beet greens.

Serves 6

braised beef short ribs

ingredients

6 pounds beef short ribs, preferably on the bone
salt and pepper
4 large onions, roughly chopped
olive oil
3 leeks, white and pale green parts only, roughly chopped
3 carrots, peeled and roughly chopped
1 can whole plum tomatoes, roughly chopped
1 whole head of garlic, cloves smashed
handful of fresh thyme sprigs
handful of fresh parsley sprigs
3 bay leaves
1 bottle Topel Cabernet Sauvignon, Meritage or Syrah wine
4 cups beef stock

directions

Season the ribs with salt and pepper and refrigerate them overnight, or for at least 8 hours.

The next day, preheat the oven to 475°. Put the short ribs, bone-side-down, in a roasting pan, and roast for 15 to 20 minutes, until the meat is lightly browned.

In a large skillet, sauté the onions in a little olive oil, until they're lightly colored. Add the leeks and carrots, and cook until they're slightly softened. Add the tomatoes, garlic, thyme, parsley and bay leaves, and sauté a little longer.

Spread the vegetables over the bottom of a roasting pan large enough to hold the ribs. Put the ribs on top of the vegetables, bone-side-up. Pour in the wine, and add enough hot stock to barely cover the ribs. Cover the pan tightly with foil and put it in the hot oven. After about 15 to 20 minutes, the braise will begin to simmer; when that happens, loosen the foil and lower the heat to 350°. Usually, after 1-½ to 2 hours, the ribs will become so tender that the meat almost falls from the bones. When the ribs are tender, uncover the pan and turn the ribs over again so that the bone side is down. Pour off and reserve all of the juices.

Increase the heat to 450° and put the ribs back in the oven to get a final browning, for about 10 minutes. Remove from the oven.

Strain the braising liquid into a bowl and press down on the solids to extract all of the juices. Put the bowl in the refrigerator to cool, which allows all the fat rise to the top. Skim if off, leaving a beautiful, rich brown sauce. Pour the sauce over the ribs and reheat before serving.

pair with topel syrah noir

Vintners Signatures

4001 highway 128,
geyserville, ca 95441
707-857-3300

www.vintnerssignatures.com

This is one of Charlie's restaurant's most
popular dishes, whether we serve the ragout
on grilled crostini, on cracker-thin pizza crust,
or our staff favorite – folded into a creamy
parmesan risotto, for our Family Meal.

Serves 4-6

wild mushroom ragout

with goat cheese over porcini mushroom polenta

chef Don Horton, Executive Chef, Charlie's at Windsor Golf Club

ingredients

Porcini Mushroom Polenta

1-½ tablespoons garlic, chopped
1 tablespoon onion, finely chopped
8 ounces butter
3-½ cups water
1 teaspoon salt
¼ teaspoon white pepper
3-½ cups Tierra Vegetables polenta
1-½ cups rehydrated and chopped dry porcini mushrooms
2 cups parmesan cheese, grated

Wild Mushroom Ragout

2 tablespoons extra virgin olive oil
4 ounces pancetta
1 medium onion, finely diced
2 cups dried porcini mushrooms, rehydrated
12 dry morel mushrooms, rehydrated
10 ounces domestic mushrooms
2 large portobello mushrooms
1 tablespoon garlic
1 tablespoon shallots
1 teaspoon fresh rosemary
1 teaspoon fresh thyme
12 basil leaves
1 tablespoon balsamic vinegar
1 teaspoon lemon zest
½ cup Pinot Noir
1 log Redwood Hill goat cheese, to top

directions make the polenta 1 day ahead

To prepare the polenta, in a saucepan, sauté the garlic and onion in the butter until the onions are soft. Add the water and bring to a boil, seasoning with salt and pepper. When the water is boiling, stir in the polenta with a wire whisk, lower the heat to a simmer, then add the chopped porcini mushrooms. Stir often for the next 20 minutes so that the polenta doesn't clump.

When the polenta is done, stir in the parmesan. Pour the polenta onto a half sheet pan and spread the mixture evenly. Allow it to cool overnight in the refrigerator, covered in plastic wrap.

To prepare the mushroom ragout, heat a large pan over medium heat. Add the olive oil and pancetta, and cook until the pancetta is caramelized. Add the onion and cook until it's tender. Chop the rehydrated and fresh mushrooms and add them to the pan. Mix well, add the remaining ingredients, and cook until the moisture is reduced by half. Keep warm.

Preheat the oven to 350°. Remove the polenta from the refrigerator and cut it into the desired shapes. Grease the bottom of a baking dish, add the polenta shapes to the dish, and warm them in the oven. Leave the oven on.

Spoon the warm ragout over the warmed polenta and crumble the goat cheese on top of the mushrooms. Return the dish to the oven until the cheese is warm, and serve.

pair with cult pinot noir

White Oak Vineyards & Winery

7505 highway 128,
healdsburg, ca 95448
707-433-8429

www.whiteoakwinery.com

This heartwarming dish became a winery favorite when it was posted on our Facebook fan page by Jesse's mother. Jesse Haney, right-hand man to our winemaker, Bill Parker, has enjoyed this dish as a family tradition for many years. He brought it to one of our vineyard pot lucks and we all decided it was especially delicious and begged for the recipe. You can prepare the stew up to two days ahead.

Serves 4-6

beef stew a la jesse

chef Dan Lucia, DL Catering

ingredients

¼ cup olive oil
1-¼ pounds stew beef, cut into 1-inch pieces
6 large garlic cloves, minced
6 cups beef stock (or canned beef broth)
1 cup strong stout beer
1 cup White Oak Merlot
2 tablespoons tomato paste
1 tablespoon sugar
1 tablespoon dried thyme
1 tablespoon Worcestershire sauce
2 bay leaves
2 tablespoons butter
3 pounds potatoes, peeled and cut into ½-inch pieces
1 large onion, chopped
2 cups carrots, peeled and cut into ½-inch pieces
2 tablespoons fresh parsley, chopped
salt and pepper, to taste

directions

Heat the olive oil in a heavy pot over medium heat. Add the beef and sauté until it's browned, about 5 minutes. Add the garlic and sauté 1 minute. Add the beef stock, beer, Merlot, tomato paste, sugar, thyme, Worcestershire sauce and bay leaves. Stir to combine. Bring the mixture to a boil, reduce the heat, cover and simmer 1 hour, stirring occasionally.

In another large pot, melt the butter over medium heat. Add the potatoes, onion and carrots, and sauté the vegetables for about 20 minutes. Set aside.

After the stew has simmered 1 hour, add the vegetables. Simmer, uncovered, until the vegetables and beef are very tender, about 40 minutes. Discard the bay leaves. Tilt the pan and spoon off the fat, and adjust the seasoning with salt and pepper, if desired.

To serve, transfer the stew to a serving bowl, sprinkle it with parsley, and serve with a loaf of crusty French bread.

pair with white oak merlot

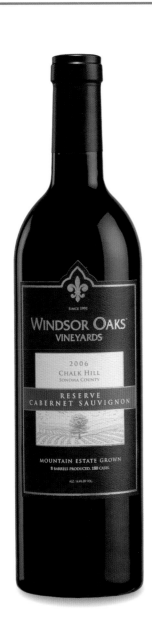

Windsor Oaks Vineyards & Winery

10810 hillview road
windsor, ca 95492
707-433-4050

www.windsoroaks.com

Our winemaker, Julie Hagler Lumgair, comes from a 5th-generation family farm and loved the barbecue grill since she was tall enough to reach it! This recipe captures the satisfying home-style feeling of harvest time lunch favored by her husband, Douglas, who planted our vineyards. The sandwich features Sonoma's finest grass-fed, free-range beef, local cheese and handmade biscuits – absolutely killer with our Cabernet Sauvignon.

Serves 6

beef short rib sandwich

chef Joe Rueter

ingredients

3 pounds beef short ribs
2 ounces grape seed oil
2 tablespoons kosher salt
1 tablespoon ground black pepper
4 ounces of your favorite barbecue sauce
3 cups shallots, thinly sliced
2 cups Windsor Oaks Reserve Cabernet Sauvignon
6 buttermilk biscuits
8 ounces aged cheddar cheese, sliced
1 bunch scallions, thinly sliced

directions preheat grill to 400°

Rub the short ribs with grape seed oil, salt and pepper. Grill the beef, turning every 2 to 3 minutes, until the outer fatty layer is golden brown. Reduce the heat to low and brush the ribs with your favorite barbecue sauce. Cook with the lid closed for 30 minutes.

Meanwhile, preheat the oven to 280°. In a roasting pan, place the sliced shallots and the wine. Transfer the grilled ribs to the roasting pan and cover tightly with foil. Bake in the oven, covered, for 2½ hours, allowing the wine's aroma to permeate the ribs until the meat is very tender and falling off the bone. Allow the ribs to cool, then remove all the meat from the bones, and discard the bones. Mix the shredded beef into the wine and shallots.

To serve, place the hot rib meat mixture on freshly baked buttermilk biscuits and top with the scallions and cheddar.

pair with windsor oaks chalk hill reserve cabernet sauvignon

desserts & sweets

Battaglini Estate Winery

2948 piner road
santa rosa, ca 95401
707-578-4091

www.battagliniwines.com

I remember my mother making these
biscotti from her grandmother's recipe.
My brother and I always complained
because the grown-ups dunked their
biscotti in wine, and we always had milk.
We thought that was so unfair!

Makes 32 biscotti

italian biscotti

chef Lucia Battaglini

ingredients

1 stick butter
1 cup almonds
1 cup walnuts
2 eggs, beaten
2 cups sugar
1 lemon rind, grated
1 orange rind, grated
1 teaspoon anise seeds
1 jigger whiskey or vermouth
4 cups flour, sifted
4 teaspoons baking power
2 teaspoons vanilla

directions preheat oven to 350°

In a small saucepan, melt the butter and set it aside to cool.

Place the almonds in a shallow pan and bake for 8 to 10 minutes, or until golden brown. Let cool. Cut the almonds and walnuts into halves or thirds. Increase the oven temperature to 350°

In a mixing bowl, beat the eggs and sugar until the mixture is light and fluffy. Mix in all the remaining ingredients, with the melted butter the last to be added. Mix well.

Divide the dough in fourths. Form 4 logs about ½-inch thick, 1-½ inches wide and 16 inches long. Place the logs on a greased and floured baking sheet, spacing them at least 2 inches apart. Bake for 20 minutes, or until the biscotti are light brown. Let cool 5 minutes. Reduce the oven temperature to 300°.

Place the biscotti on a cutting board. With a serrated knife, slice the cookies diagonally at a 45° angle, about ½-inch thick. Place them on a baking sheet and return them to the oven for 10 to 15 minutes to dry. Let cool, then enjoy, or store in a tightly covered container.

pair with battaglini chardonnay

Camellia Cellars

57 front street
healdsburg, ca 95448
707-433-1290

www.camelliacellars.com

I was born on my father's birthday, Nov. 5. Since I'm always working "A Wine & Food Affair," to celebrate, I often prepare our birthday cake to share with everyone. This year's selection is a moist, dense cake, almost like a torte. It freezes well (un-frosted). I adapted this recipe from the "Nantucket Open House Cookbook" by Sarah Leah Chase. I use locally grown organic walnuts and farm-fresh organic eggs. There's something about chocolate, walnuts and espresso that just screams to be paired with our luscious Cabernet Sauvignon.

Serves 8-10

chocolate-espresso
cake with walnuts
chef Chris Lewand

ingredients

Cake
1 cup sugar
¼ cup water
1 tablespoon instant espresso powder
6 ounces semi-sweet chocolate chips
1 ½ teaspoons vanilla extract
½ cup unsalted butter, room temperature
8 large eggs, separated
1 ⅓ cups walnuts
1 slice white bread, crusts removed
pinch salt

Frosting
6 ounces semi-sweet chocolate chips
⅓ cup water
1 tablespoon instant espresso powder
1 cup unsalted butter, room temperature
3 large egg yolks
¾ cup powdered sugar
walnuts, ground, for garnish
chocolate-covered coffee beans, for garnish

directions preheat oven to 350°

To prepare the cake, butter 2 9-inch round cake pans and line them with parchment paper. Butter the paper and dust with flour, and shake out the excess.

In a small saucepan, add the sugar, water and espresso powder and bring to a boil, stirring constantly. Add the chocolate and vanilla, whisking until the chocolate is melted and smooth. Allow to cool.

Cream the butter in a mixer until it's very light and fluffy. Beat in the egg yolks 1 at a time. Gradually beat in the cooled chocolate mixture. In a food processor, process the walnuts and bread with the steel blade. Stir the walnut mixture into the chocolate mixture.

Beat the egg whites with the salt, until stiff peaks form (but not dry), then gently fold them into the chocolate mixture. Divide the batter evenly into the 2 pans, and bake for 25 to 30 minutes, until the cake edges pull away from the pans slightly. Don't over-bake. Cool 15 minutes in the pans, then invert onto a wire rack to cool completely.

To prepare the frosting, put the chocolate, water and espresso powder in a small saucepan and heat, whisking until the chocolate is melted and smooth. Refrigerate until it's slightly chilled. Beat the butter in a mixer until very light and fluffy. Beat in the egg yolks, 1 at a time. Gradually beat in the chilled chocolate mixture, then the powdered sugar. Keep beating until the frosting is thick and spreadable.

Frost the top of 1 cake, top with the second cake, and frost the top and sides. Garnish with the ground walnuts and candy coffee beans. Serve slightly chilled.

pair with camellia cellars cabernet sauvignon

Foppiano
Vineyards

12707 old redwood highway
healdsburg, ca 95448
707-433-7272

www.foppiano.com

This is a favorite to serve for birthday parties and special occasions. The terrine is rich yet light, and with a small change in the custard and nuts, the wine-pairing possibilities are endless!

Serves 10–12

chocolate terrine

with crème anglaise

chef Chris Bertsche

ingredients

Terrine
canola oil
12 ounces semi-sweet or bittersweet chocolate
9 ounces unsalted butter
4 large eggs, separated
4 large egg yolks
1-⅓ cups powdered sugar
⅓ cup cocoa powder
½ cup plus 1 tablespoon heavy cream
2 teaspoons sugar
1 cup pistachios, shelled, toasted and chopped

Crème Anglaise
1 cup milk
1 cup heavy cream
7 tablespoons sugar
½ vanilla bean, split and seeds scraped
(retain pod)
5 large egg yolks

directions prepare 1 day ahead

To prepare the terrine, oil a 12-inch loaf pan, line it with plastic wrap and set it aside. Melt the chocolate and butter together in a double boiler over warm water, stirring slowly. Remove the chocolate from the heat and let it cool until it's warm to the touch. Stir in the 8 egg yolks. Sift together the powdered sugar and cocoa powder and stir into the chocolate mixture.

With an electric mixer, whip the cream to soft peaks, then put it in the refrigerator while you beat the egg whites. With clean beaters, beat the egg whites and sugar until soft peaks form.

To prepare the crème anglaise, in a saucepan, combine the milk, cream and 4 tablespoons of sugar. Add the vanilla bean seeds and pod to the mixture, and heat on medium to dissolve the sugar, and then bring to a simmer. Remove the pan from the heat and let the vanilla infuse for about 30 minutes.

Place a metal bowl over an ice bath. Reheat the cream mixture until it's warm. Meanwhile, whisk the yolks with the remaining sugar in a medium bowl, until the mixture thickens and lightens in color. Whisking constantly, gradually pour about ⅓ of the warm cream mixture into the yolks to temper them. Return the mixture to the saucepan and cook over low heat, stirring constantly with a wooden spoon, for about 10 minutes, or until the custard thickens and coats the back of the spoon.

Pour the custard into the iced metal bowl, stirring constantly, until cooled. Strain the custard into another bowl and refrigerate for at least 2 hours. Fold the egg whites into the chocolate mixture, and then fold in the whipped cream. Pour this mixture into the loaf pan and refrigerate, covered with plastic wrap, for at least 12 hours.

To serve, remove the terrine from the pan and plastic, and using a hot knife, slice it into ¼-inch-thick pieces. Place on a bed of custard and garnish with the pistachios.

pair with foppiano petite sirah

Fritz Underground Winery

24691 dutcher creek road
cloverdale, ca 95425
707-894-3389

www.fritzwinery.com

Decadent, chewy, ooey-gooey dark chocolate brownies are ideal for pairing with our Late Harvest Zinfandel. We baked these brownies at the winery for years, and they're always a hit. As you bake them, the smell infuses the kitchen, bringing friends and family from near and far together to indulge in this special treat.

Makes 16 pieces

decadently dark cherry
chocolate brownies
with fritz late harvest zinfandel

chef Julie Herson, Salt Side Down Chocolates

ingredients

2 cups dried cherries
7 ounces Fritz Late Harvest Zinfandel
butter for greasing pan
½ cup whole wheat pastry flour
⅓ cup Dutch process cocoa powder, plus more for dusting
½ teaspoon fine-grain sea salt
2 teaspoons baking powder
10.5 ounces 65% dark chocolate chips/chunks
5-½ tablespoons unsalted butter
2 cups dark brown sugar
4 large eggs
½ cup crème fraiche or sour cream
1 cup chocolate chips/chunks

directions start 1 day ahead

A day before baking the brownies, place the cherries in a medium bowl and add the Zinfandel. Cover the mixture and set aside, stirring every 12 hours until you're ready to use it.

The next day, preheat the oven to 325° and place a rack in the top third. Butter and line a 13-inch by 9-inch rectangular baking dish with parchment paper. Sift the flour, cocoa powder, salt and baking powder into a bowl and set aside.

Make a double boiler by placing a stainless steel bowl over a small pan of gently simmering water; the bottom of the bowl should not touch the water. Place the 10.5 ounces of chocolate into this bowl, along with the butter and sugar. Stir just until the chocolate has melted and the ingredients come together into a mass.

Transfer the chocolate to the bowl of an electric mixer and allow the mixture to cool (cool enough that it won't cook the eggs when you add them). Mix on slow and add the eggs, 1 at a time, letting each get incorporated before adding the next. Scrape down the sides of the bowl with a spatula a few times along the way. Add the flour mixture and stir by hand until combined, then add the crème fraiche, remaining chocolate, and the cherries with the Zinfandel. Stir until just combined.

Spoon the mixture into the prepared pan and bake for about 1 hour, or until just set. The center of the brownie should be set and not wobbly. Allow it to cool completely in the pan. You can cover the pan tightly with plastic wrap and the brownie will keep for a couple days. I recommend chilling it before slicing if you want small, precise squares. Also keep a tall glass of warm water on hand to wash your knife between each cut. Enjoy at room temperature, dusted with a bit of cocoa powder.

pair with fritz late harvest zinfandel

Geyser Peak Winery

22281 chianti road
geyserville, ca 95441
707-857-9400

www.geyserpeakwinery.com

Before starting this recipe, purchase chocolate cups (also called snobinettes, though you don't have to be a snob to enjoy them). These are mini dark chocolate cups that can be filled with all sorts of sweet things, including this chocolate mousse and port caramel. Chocolate cups can be found at some gourmet grocers and bakeries, and on online at marquefoods.com and amazon.com. Also have two pastry bags ready.

Makes 36 cups

chocolate

mousse cups

with port "caramel"

chef Jesse McQuarrie, Feast Catering

ingredients

Mousse
8 ounces bittersweet chocolate
¼ cup brewed espresso
2 tablespoons Grand Marnier
1 cup heavy cream
2 eggs, separated
6 large egg whites, at room temperature
1 pinch cream of tartar
2 tablespoons sugar

Caramel
2 cups sugar
4 tablespoons water
1 750-ml bottle of port
36 chocolate cups

directions

To prepare the mousse, place the chocolate in the food processor bowl, fitted with a steel blade. Pulse until the chocolate is very finely chopped and leave the chocolate in the bowl.

In a small saucepan, combine the espresso, Grand Marnier and 2 tablespoons of the cream, and bring to a boil. Turn on the food processor and add the hot liquid to the processor, with the blades running. Process until the chocolate has melted. Stop the processor, scrape down the sides, and continue to process until smooth. Add the 2 egg yolks and process until the mixture is blended. Scrape it into a large bowl.

In the bowl of a stand mixer fitted with a whisk attachment, or in a large bowl, beat the egg whites on medium speed. When they foam, add the cream of tartar and continue to beat on medium speed, while you slowly stream in the sugar. Beat until the egg whites form medium peaks. Fold into the chocolate base in 2 additions.

In the same mixer, beat the remaining cream until it forms soft peaks, and fold into the mousse. Spoon the mixture into a pastry bag to pipe into the chocolate cups.

To prepare the caramel, mix the sugar and water in a large bowl and add it to a heated sauté pan. Cook over medium-high heat until golden, stirring constantly. Take the pan off the heat and carefully add the port. Stir, and put the pan back on the heat. Reduce the caramel until it has a syrupy consistency. Refrigerate until the caramel is cold, then put it into a pastry bag.

To serve the cups, pipe the mousse into the chocolate cups, then add the caramel on top for color. Enjoy!

pair with geyser peak tawny port

Highlands Resort

14000 woodland drive
guerneville, ca 95446
707-869-0333

www.highlandsresort.com

We are "world famous" for our muffins. We bake them fresh on the weekends – apple, pineapple upside-down, orange-bittersweet chocolate, pecan sticky, just to name a few. Even our e-mail address is muffins@ highlandsresort.com. About 14 years ago, we wanted to create a recipe for an apple muffin that was moist and had a great apple flavor. Gravenstein apples are great baking apples and are perfect in this recipe. The sour cream gives the muffins a tender and moist crumb, and the streusel topping adds a nice crunch.

Serves 12

apple
streusel muffins

chef Kenneth McLean

ingredients

Batter
¼ cup butter
1 cup sour cream
2 large eggs
1-½ cups all-purpose flour
½ cup granulated sugar
2 teaspoons baking powder
1 teaspoon ground cinnamon
¼ teaspoon ground allspice
¼ teaspoon baking soda
¼ teaspoon salt
½ cup chopped walnuts
1 medium apple, cored and diced (we use Granny Smith or Gravenstein; peeling is optional)

Topping
3 tablespoons brown sugar
3 tablespoons granulated sugar
½ teaspoon ground cinnamon

directions preheat oven to 350°

Spray a muffin pan with non-stick spray.

To prepare the batter, melt the butter in a heat-proof dish in a microwave oven, and pour the butter into a large bowl. Allow it to cool slightly. Add the sour cream and eggs, mixing well with a whisk.

Sift together and stir in the flour, sugar, baking powder, cinnamon, allspice, baking soda and salt. Stir until just barely mixed. Fold in the walnuts and apple. With muffins, you don't want to over-mix; just barely blend the ingredients together. Spoon the batter into the greased muffin cups.

To prepare the topping, mix the brown sugar, granulated sugar and cinnamon together in a small bowl and sprinkle the mixture on top of the muffin batter. Bake for 20 to 25 minutes, until the muffins are firm to the touch and golden brown. Serve warm.

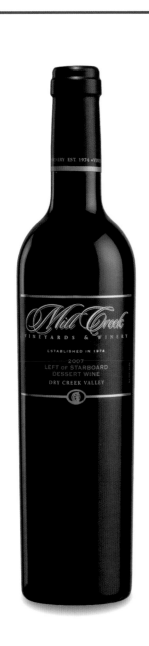

Mill Creek Vineyards & Winery

1401 westside road
healdsburg, ca 95448
707-431-2121

www.millcreekwinery.com

Chocolate and raspberries deliciously complement each other in this dessert dish. Use plastic squeeze bottles to add the crepe batter to the pan, and the chocolate ganache to the finished crepes.

Serves 6-10

scrumptious chocolate-raspberry

crepes

chef Lydia Henrikson, Zakuski Catering

ingredients

Crepes
¾ cup all-purpose flour
1 teaspoon baking powder
½ teaspoon salt
2 tablespoons sugar
2 eggs
⅔ cup milk
⅓ cup water
½ teaspoon vanilla

Raspberry Syrup
2 pints fresh raspberries
1 teaspoon butter
3 cups sugar

Dark Chocolate Ganache
2 cups dark chocolate pistoles
(64% cacao is best)
1 cup heavy whipping cream
1 ounce sugar
1 ounce butter

directions

To prepare the crepes, whisk together all the dry ingredients in a mixing bowl and set aside. In a separate bowl, whisk the eggs and add the milk, water and vanilla. Slowly incorporate the dry ingredients into the wet ingredients. Let the batter sit for at least 30 minutes to fully hydrate all the dry ingredients. You can also refrigerate this overnight to make a more beautiful and smooth batter.

Put the batter into a squeeze bottle. Cook the crepes in an 8-inch non-stick pan. Heat the pan on medium and brush it lightly with butter. Squeeze a 3-inch-diameter amount of batter into the center of the pan. Swirl the batter around to coat the pan evenly. When the crepe looks dry on top, flip it to nicely brown the other side. Several crepes can be made and stacked; they won't stick together.

To prepare the raspberry syrup, in a saucepan, crush the berries, add the butter and bring the mixture to a boil on high heat. When the berries are at a full rolling boil that cannot be stirred down, add the sugar all at once. Boil hard for 1 minute.

To prepare the ganache, bring the cream to scalding point and pour it over the chocolate pistoles. Stir only several times; do not whip or over-agitate the mixture. When the chocolate is fully melted, add the sugar and butter. Put the ganache in a squeeze bottle with a small tip. The ganache will remain at a nice coating consistency if you use it right away, after it cools slightly. If you need to reheat it, put the squeeze bottle in warm water.

To serve, place a crepe on the plate and squeeze the desired amount of ganache over it. Roll the crepe into a cylinder shape, and spoon raspberry sauce on top.

pair with mill creek vineyards left of starboard port-style wine

Old Crocker Inn

1126 old crocker inn road
cloverdale, ca 95425
707-894-4000

www.oldcrockerinn.com

This easy, delicious recipe came from
a friend whose mom in the title was a
wonderful cook in the mid-20th century.
It has been a favorite here at the inn
and in places as far-flung as Sarajevo
and Kabul, when blueberries are
available in local markets.

Serves 8-10

fernie's
blueberry torte

chef Marcia Babb

ingredients

Crust
1 cup flour
pinch of salt
2 tablespoons sugar
1 stick unsalted butter, chilled
1 tablespoon white or apple vinegar

Filling
1 cup sugar
2 tablespoons flour
½ teaspoon cinnamon
2 pints fresh blueberries (3-4 cups, depending on berry size)
powdered sugar, for dusting (optional)
mint sprigs, for garnish

directions preheat oven to 400°

To prepare the crust, combine the first 3 ingredients in a bowl and work in the butter and vinegar with your fingers or a pastry fork (or pulse in a food processor) until you have coarse crumbs. Spread and pat the mixture into a 9-inch, removable-bottom cake pan and about 1 inch up the sides.

To prepare the filling, in a small bowl, combine the sugar, flour and cinnamon. Wash and dry the blueberries, and gently blend 3 cups of them into the sugar/flour mixture. Add this mixture to the crust, and bake about 50 minutes, until the filling bubbles and the crust is lightly browned. Remove the pan from the oven and sprinkle the remaining blueberries over the top. Cool and dust with powdered sugar, if desired. Garnish with mint sprigs and serve.

pair with your favorite late harvest zinfandel

Pech Merle Winery

24505 chianti road
cloverdale, ca 95425
707-585-9599

www.pechmerlewinery.com

The name of this recipe answers the question: Why is this dessert so special? It's an easy-to-prepare chocolate cake made more decadent by the addition of Zinfandel.

Serves 12

because I'm zinfully rich, that's why

chef Dan Lucia, DL Catering

ingredients

1 cup Pech Merle Zinfandel
12 ounces semi-sweet chocolate
1-½ cups butter
2-½ cups sugar
6 eggs
2 tablespoons vanilla extract
2-½ cups flour
1 teaspoon sea salt

directions preheat oven to 325°

In a small saucepan, reduce the Zinfandel by half, let it cool and set it aside. In a double boiler, add the chocolate and butter and cook over medium heat until both ingredients are melted. Add the sugar and remove the pan from the heat.

In a mixing bowl, beat the eggs and add the chocolate/butter mixture. Stir to combine, and add the reduced Zinfandel and vanilla extract. Stir again. Add the flour and salt, and pour the mixture into a lightly greased 9-inch by 12-inch sheet pan. Bake for approximately 20 minutes, or until the top of the cake has a thin skin on top.

pair with pech merle dry creek valley zinfandel, l' entrée dry creek valley zinfandel or alexander valley cabernet sauvignon

Robert Rue
Vineyard

1406 wood road
fulton, ca 95439
707-578-1601

www.robertruevineyard.com

If I wanted to impress someone (like a new beau), this was the recipe I chose ... and it always worked! This is an easy and delicious flourless chocolate cake with the most sinful Zinfandel cherry sauce.

Serves 8

zinful delight

chef Kathy Bradley

ingredients

Cake
2 ounces unsweetened chocolate,
broken into small pieces
4 ounces semi-sweet chocolate, broken into small pieces
9 tablespoons unsalted butter, room temperature
¾ cup sugar
3 tablespoons almonds, ground
5 large eggs, separated
pinch of salt

Sauce
½ cup Robert Rue Zinfandel
½ cup sugar
zest from ½ lemon
½ pound dried, pitted cherries

directions preheat oven to 350°

To prepare the cake, line the bottom of a round, 9-inch springform pan with buttered waxed paper, then flour the pan, shaking out the excess.

Place both chocolates in a double boiler over simmering water, and stir until the chocolate is melted. Pour it into a bowl and let it cool for about 3 minutes. Add the butter to the chocolate in pieces, stirring to incorporate, then add ½ cup of sugar and the almonds. Continue stirring and add the egg yolks, 1 at a time.

Beat the egg whites and salt until they form soft peaks, then gradually add the remaining ¼ cup of sugar and beat until the egg whites hold their shape. Fold, in thirds, the egg whites into the chocolate mixture. Pour the mixture into the prepared the pan and bake 35 minutes. Allow the cake to cool on a wire rack. Then remove the sides of the springform pan, invert the cake onto rack, and remove the bottom of the pan and the waxed paper.

To prepare the sauce, place the wine, sugar and lemon zest in a saucepan and reduce the liquid, over medium heat, to a fairly thick consistency. Add the dried cherries to the reduction, and let the sauce rest so that the cherries rehydrate in the liquid.

To serve, cut individual slices of the cake, place them on dessert plates, and drizzle the sauce as liberally as you like.

pair with robert rue vineyard zinfandel

Rued Vineyards & Winery

3850 dry creek road
healdsburg, ca 95448
707-433-3261

www.ruedvineyards.com

I love this recipe as a dessert after a heavy meal or on a buffet as a sweet treat. It's wonderful when local berries are in season.

Serves 8

lemon ricotta tart

chef Tracy Bidia

ingredients

Lemon Curd
8 egg yolks
1 cup sugar
zest of 2 lemons, finely grated
½ cup plus 2 tablespoons lemon juice
⅛ teaspoon salt
1-¼ sticks unsalted butter

Shortbread
1 cup butter
⅓ cup powdered sugar
1-¼ cups flour
½ cup ricotta cheese
2 cups fresh berries

directions

To prepare the curd, whisk the yolks, sugar, lemon zest and lemon juice in a heat-proof bowl set over a pan of simmering water. Continue whisking until the mixture becomes thick and coats the back of a spoon. Remove from the heat, and add the salt and butter 1 piece at a time, mixing until smooth. Refrigerate for 1 hour.

To prepare the shortbread, preheat the oven to 350°. Cream the butter, powdered sugar and flour until smooth. Press the dough into cupcake tins and bake for 15 to 20 minutes. Let the shortbread cool and turn them out gently.

Mix ½ cup of lemon curd with the ricotta cheese. Using a pastry bag, pipe the lemon curd on half of a shortbread crust, and pipe the lemon ricotta mixture on the other half. Sprinkle with powdered sugar and garnish with berries of your choice.

pair with rued russian river valley chardonnay

Russian River Vineyards

5700 gravenstein highway north
forestville, ca 95436
707-887-3344

www.russianrivervineyards.com

We served this dessert to our wine club
members and it was so popular that we
decided to add it to the menu at our Corks
at Russian River Vineyards restaurant.

Serves 10

desserts & sweets

brioche & pinot
bread pudding
chef Jerry Mitchell

ingredients

12 medium eggs
⅛ cup ground allspice
1⁄16 cup nutmeg
1⁄16 cup cinnamon, plus more for sprinkling
¼ cup Russian River Vineyards Pinot Noir
1⁄16 cup vanilla
1 quart whole milk
1 cup raisins
1 cup raspberries
2-½ cups brioche or egg bread loaf, crusts removed and cut into ½-inch cubes
2 cups light brown sugar, plus more for sprinkling
olive oil

directions preheat oven to 300°

In a large mixing bowl, combine the eggs, allspice, nutmeg, cinnamon, Pinot Noir, vanilla, milk, raisins and raspberries. Stir well.

Grease a baking pan with olive oil and add the bread cubes, spreading them around evenly. Pour the egg/Pinot Noir mixture over the bread cubes and let stand for a few minutes, allowing the bread to absorb the wet mixture. Spread the 2 cups of brown sugar on top.

Place the brioche pan in a larger, shallow pan and add warm water to the larger pan so that the level is halfway up the side of the brioche pan. Carefully place the water bath pan in the oven and bake the bread pudding for 1 hour, until it's lightly brown on top and the custard underneath has set.

To serve, sprinkle the top of the cooked bread pudding with cinnamon and sugar, and cut it into ½-inch-thick slices. Top with creme anglaise, if desired, and serve warm.

pair with russian river vineyards pinot noir

Souverain

26150 asti road
cloverdale, ca 95425
707-265-5490

www.souverain.com

Amaretti are Italian almond cookies, and you can find them in gourmet markets and at many Italian delicatessens. If you can't find Green Zebra figs, substitute with the widely available Mission figs.

Serves 8

desserts & sweets

caramelized green-striped
zebra figs

with amaretti cookie crust & white chocolate custard cream

chef Maurine Sarjeant

vegi

ingredients

Custard Cream
¾ cup sugar
⅛ teaspoon salt
2 tablespoons cornstarch
3-½ cups half-and-half
3 large egg yolks
1 tablespoon unsalted butter
¾ cup chopped white chocolate

Figs
4 tablespoons granulated sugar
1-¼ cups water
10 fresh figs, quartered
1 vanilla bean, scraped

Amaretti Crust
8 5-inch individual tart pans
1 10-ounce package amarretti cookies, ground
6 ounces cold butter, grated
¼ cup powdered sugar

directions

To prepare the custard cream, combine the sugar, salt and cornstarch in a saucepan. Slowly whisk in the half-and-half, then the eggs. Simmer the cream over medium-high heat, whisking constantly yet gently.

Reduce the heat and continue whisking gently, until the mixture is thick enough to coat the back of a spoon, about 5 minutes. Add the white chocolate to a large bowl, and strain the cream mixture into the bowl, through a fine mesh strainer. Stir until all the chocolate is melted. Add the butter and stir until all the ingredients are mixed.

Press a sheet of plastic wrap directly onto the surface of the cream and refrigerate for 3 hours.

To prepare the crust, combine all the ingredients in a food processor, and pulse until well blended. Press the mixture into individual tart pans and set aside.

To prepare the figs, in a saucepan, bring the sugar and water to a boil over medium heat. Add the vanilla bean seeds and figs. Simmer for 30 minutes, or until the mixture becomes thick and syrupy.

After the cream is sufficiently chilled, spoon it onto the amaretti crusts in the tart pans, top each with a spoonful of fig mixture, and serve.

pair with souverain dessert syrah

recipe index by winery and lodging

the wineries

recipe index by winery and lodging

the wineries continued

recipe index by winery and lodging

the wineries continued

recipe index by winery and lodging

the wineries continued & the lodgings

the lodgings

onward and upward...

Now in its 33rd year, the Wine Road has grown from the original nine founding winery members to a spirited collection of 165 wineries and 50 lodgings throughout the Alexander, Dry Creek and Russian River valleys of Northern Sonoma County. As our association continues to grow, the Wine Road continues to update its web site to make it a one-stop resource for planning your visit to wine country. Wine Road is located just one easy hour's drive north of the Golden Gate Bridge. We enjoy the grandeur of the Pacific Ocean, stately redwoods, picturesque towns and rolling vineyards, all easily accessed along quiet country roads. If you live locally, we hope you treat yourself to a staycation and enjoy what's in your backyard. We call it...Heaven Condensed.

now that's the ticket...

The Wine Road now offers you a great way to save while visiting our member wineries and lodgings: "Ticket to the Wine Road."

Log onto wineroad.com and click on the TICKET link to see the list of wineries and lodgings that are participating in the program. You can buy a one-day pass for $25 or a three-day pass for $50; simply select the dates you want to use the pass when you place your order. Currently, 55 wineries and 12 lodgings have special offers, complimentary tasting, barrel samples or other fun offers for "Ticket" holders. When you order, you will see that our event weekends are blackout dates, and the "Ticket" will not work for groups of eight or more. Check it out – Ticket to the Wine Road.

just being sociable...

Be sure to follow us on facebook.com/wineroad – we keep it fun with give-aways, insider scoops and featured members, and we love it when YOU tell our followers YOUR favorite spots along the Wine Road. We keep fans up to speed on area events, wine releases and last-minute specials. We post seasonal videos so that you can see what's happening along the Wine Road throughout the year, and our "Life of Riley" has documented the month-by-month changes in a single vine throughout the year.

events

Annual **Wine Road** Events

Winter Wineland
January - Martin Luther King Jr Birthday Weekend

A great opportunity to meet winemakers and taste limited-production wines. Enjoy a weekend of wine tasting, winemaker chats, winery tours and seminars.

Tickets are available in advance, online: $40 for the weekend, $30 for Sunday only, and $10 for designated drivers. Once online tickets sales end, prices at the door are $50 weekend, $40 Sunday only and $10 designated drivers. Online tickets go on sale the previous November at www.wineroad.com.

Barrel Tasting
March - First two weekends

A chance to sample wines from the barrel and talk with winemakers. It's also a special opportunity to purchase "futures," often at a discount. Come back to the winery after the wine is bottled (typically 12-16 months later) and pick up your purchase. The production of many member wineries is so limited that buying futures is your only chance to purchase the wine you like.

Tickets are available in advance, online: $20 per person, per weekend. Once online ticket sales end, prices at the door are $30 per person, per weekend.

A Wine & Food Affair
November - The first full weekend

Our premier event: A full weekend of wine and food pairings, complete with the current volume of "Tasting Along the Wine Road" cookbook and event logo glass. All participating wineries will have a recipe for a favorite dish in the cookbook, which they will prepare both days for you to sample, paired with the perfect wine. Many Wine Road lodgings also provide recipes for inclusion in the cookbook.

Tickets are available in advance, online: $65 for the weekend, $45 for Sunday only and $25 for designated drivers. Online tickets go on sale the previous September at www.wineroad.com. There are NO tickets sold at the door for this event

For details on these annual events and other wine country festivities sponsored by our members, visit
www.wineroad.com

our AVAs (american viticultural areas)

Alexander Valley

Total acres: 32,536 • Vineyard acres: 15,000 • Number of wineries: 49, growing 23 grape varieties

This valley is named for the 19th-century pioneer Cyrus Alexander, explorer of Northern Sonoma County and resident of the area. Alexander Valley flanks the Russian River from Cloverdale to Healdsburg. Along the heavily graveled benchlands, one finds world-class Cabernet Sauvignon grapes. Considered one of the most diverse grapegrowing regions in California, the valley is also planted to Chardonnay, Zinfandel, Merlot, Sauvignon Blanc and other varieties, which prosper on the long, undulating valley floor and hillsides.

Forty years ago, prunes and walnuts reigned supreme in the Alexander Valley, and the flatlands were dotted with bovine herds. Today, the lowlands produce Chardonnays that achieve a rich and flavorful ripeness. The warmer northern end of the valley favors Cabernet Sauvignon, Zinfandel, Merlot and newcomers like French Syrah and Italian Sangiovese. Vineyards that scale the hillsides surrounding the valley floor provide grapes with deep and complex flavors. Hunt around and you can also still find some of the juiciest, most succulent prunes you've ever tasted.

Dry Creek Valley

Total acres: 78,387 • Vineyard acres: 9,000 • Number of wineries: 60-plus, growing 26 grape varieties

Dry Creek Valley's history of grapegrowing and winemaking is among the longest in California, with roots beginning more than 135 years ago. The precise blend of climate, soil and exposure that produces grapes of singular quality and character is the true allure of the region.

The valley is approximately 16 miles long and 2 miles wide. It is framed on the western edge by rugged mountain ridges rimmed with redwoods and evergreens. The climate reflects both coastal and inland influences and is classified as Region II on the UC Davis scale. The proximity to the ocean is tempered by the intervening coastal hills breached by the Russian River. While Dry Creek Valley experiences coastal cooling in the late afternoon during summer, fog rarely enters the valley until after nightfall. The climate is warmer in the north and cooler in the south, allowing for diversity of grapegrowing.

Dry Creek Valley is recognized as a premium winegrowing region in California, and Zinfandel is the signature varietal. However, the diversity of the soil encourages the production of a broad range of top-quality Bordeaux and Mediterranean grape varieties.

Russian River Valley

Total acres: 126,600 • Vineyard acres: 10,000 • Number of wineries: 130, growing 30 grape varieties

What makes Russian River Valley stand out is its climate. This low-lying flat plain extends south and west of Healdsburg as it winds its way along the Russian River and descends to meet the Pacific at Jenner, then makes it way toward the Golden Gate Bridge, ending about 55 miles north of this landmark. This area thrives from the coastal influences of the Pacific Ocean, which makes it an exceptional place for growing cool-climate grapes like Pinot Noir and Chardonnay.

The Russian River Valley is so expansive that it has two smaller appellations within it: Green Valley and Chalk Hill. Green Valley is one of the smallest appellations in the county, nestled in the southwest corner of the Russian River Valley. This area is greatly affected by the cooling coastal elements, which benefit the cool-climate grapes that flourish in these conditions. Chalk Hill, named for the volcanic soil that makes up the area, is a unique little gem known for its outstanding wines. By being situated in the northwest corner of Russian River Valley, it has warmer temperatures that allow Merlot and Cabernet Sauvignon to thrive.

Russian River Valley Chardonnays are exceptional, slightly more lean and refined than those of Alexander Valley, yet the fruit is still developed enough to sustain months in oak barrels, creating depth and complexity. Pinot Noir brought this area international acclaim. Whereas most red wines focus on flavor, Pinot Noir is about an alluring, sensual, velvety mouth-feel. It is a textural delight that can only be found where morning fog turns to warm afternoons, so that grape maturity is achieved without loss of depth and suppleness.

our AVAs (american viticultural areas)

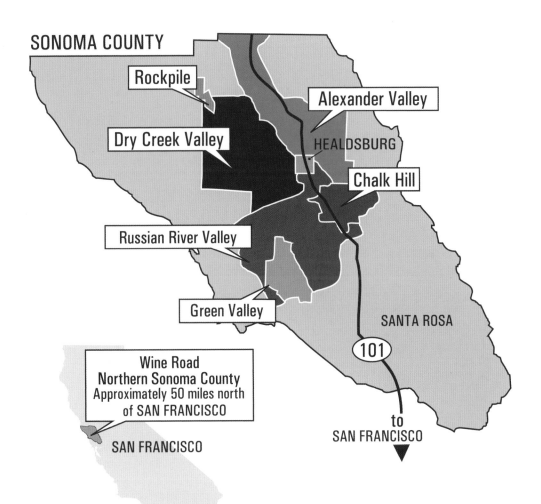

SONOMA COUNTY

Rockpile

Alexander Valley

Dry Creek Valley

HEALDSBURG

Chalk Hill

Russian River Valley

Green Valley

SANTA ROSA

101

Wine Road
Northern Sonoma County
Approximately 50 miles north
of SAN FRANCISCO

SAN FRANCISCO

to
SAN FRANCISCO
▼

Wine Road Northern Sonoma County

wine road gives back

In May 2010, Wine Road Executive Director Beth Costa and then-President Nancy Woods presented the Redwood Empire Food Bank with a portion of the proceeds from this year's 32nd annual Barrel Tasting. More than 100 wineries located in the Dry Creek, Russian River and Alexander valleys threw open their cellar doors to celebrate the 2010 Barrel Tasting, and during the two weekends, raised an impressive $28,000 for the Food Bank.

The Redwood Empire Food Bank serves 60,000 people in Sonoma, Mendocino, Lake, Humboldt and Del Norte counties each month, including children, seniors and working families.

"The Wine Road is proud to support the Redwood Empire Food Bank and in turn, those in need in the community," Costa says. "We are so proud of the fact that our contributions to this organization over the last five years now total more than $120,000. Our members can truly be proud."

This year's $28,000 donation was a combination of $25,000 from the Wine Road and $3,000 from customers who donated when ordering tickets.

David Goodman of REFB, Nancy Woods and
Beth Costa of Wine Road and Lee Bickley of REFB.

In addition to the donation from Barrel Tasting, $1 for every ticket sold for A Wine & Food Affair is donated to the Redwood Empire Food Bank. For more information about REFB or to make a donation, please log onto www.refb.com.

it's good to be green...

The winds of change are blowing along the Wine Road...

We're looking at our surroundings and finding ways that we can make sure our environmental impact is as minimal as possible.

Starting in 2008, the Wine Road began reducing plastic waste by providing event attendees with Calistoga drinking water from refillable, multi-gallon containers. Guests dispense water directly into their event wine glasses, instead of drinking from individual plastic bottles, or using paper cups.

After the events, these water containers are returned to the Calistoga Beverage Co. to be refilled and used time and time again.

To reduce paper consumption, Wine Road no longer mails event invitations to the thousands of people on our mailing list. Instead, we reach out to our guests via online invitations. We count on everyone to help us spread the word about our events and happenings, and have added "share" buttons to our web site so that you can easily e-mail all the news to friends and family.

In addition, we no longer print and mail tickets; guests simply order online and print e-tickets at home. Detailed event programs are available in PDF format on our web site.

Rather than mailing newsletters, we keep visitors updated via online sources; follow us on Facebook and Twitter. Sign up for our e-mail news, which we send out monthly, with lodging specials and event information from our members.

For details on these annual events and other wine country festivities sponsored by our members, visit www.wineroad.com